Tel Aviv University   אוניברסיטת תל-אביב

Lester and Sally Entin Faculty of Humanities

The Stephen Roth Institute
for the Study of Contemporary Antisemitism
and Racism

Antisemitism Worldwide
2001/2

Anti-Defamation League

World Jewish Congress

The Stephen Roth Institute welcomes the contribution of studies on antisemitism and racism in different periods, as well as book reviews, for inclusion in *Antisemitism Worldwide*. Manuscripts, for IBM-compatible computers, should be sent to the Stephen Roth Institute, Wiener Library, Tel Aviv University, POB 39040, Tel Aviv 69978, or e-mailed as an attached Word file to anti@post.tau.ac.il.

The Stephen Roth Institute for the Study of Contemporary Antisemitism and Racism is located in the Wiener Library, at Tel Aviv University. Its extensive database monitors antisemitism and racism throughout the world, serving researchers and community, governmental and organizational workers in Israel and abroad, as well as human rights organizations and groups fighting racism.

The Institute operates in cooperation with the Anti-Defamation League (ADL), headed by its international director Abraham Foxman. The ADL is known for its 80-year-long struggle for civil rights. The World Jewish Congress (WJC), the umbrella organization of Jewish communities in 80 countries around the world, participates in the Institute's work as well. The WJC, under President Edgar Bronfman and Secretary-General Dr. Avi Beker, is represented in Israel by Ms. Simona Kedmi. The Institute's data collection was assisted by the Coordination Forum for Countering Antisemitism, under Deputy Minister of Foreign Affairs Rabbi Michael Melchior.

Institute Staff and Volunteers

Ruth Becker
Hanna Benda
Ruth Braude
Fani Englard
Bella Giladi
Arzia Hershberg
Nesia Hordes
Shulamit Kaplan

Salman Mualam
Rosita Nevo
Fania Pizov
Amir Rom
Yemima Silberman
Chana Singer
Gabi Singer
Wanda Wasserman

This volume is dedicated to the memory of our beloved staff member FANIA PIZOV, who passed away in December 2002.

AUTHORS AND CONTRIBUTORS

Manuel Abramovicz

Centre pour l'égalité des chances et la lutte contre le racisme, Belgium

Tina Ader

Embassy of Israel, Germany

Andreas Angersdorfer

University Regensburg, Germany

Claudio Avruj

DAIA, Argentina

Alejandro Baer Mieses

Spain

Alberto Benasuly

B'nai B'rith, Spain

Marisa Braylan

DAIA, Argentina

Jean-Yves Camus

Centre européen de recherche et d'action sur le racisme et l'antisémitisme (CERA), Paris, France

Moses Constantinis

Central Board of Jewish Communities, Greece

Renée Dayan-Shabot

Tribuna Israelita, Mexico

Herbert Donner

Comite Central Israelita, Uruguay

Gail Gans

ADL, New York

Adriana Goldstaub

Fondazione Centro di Documentazione Ebraica Contemporanea, Italy

Goethe Institute	Tel Aviv
Pietro Greppi	Italy
Gustavo Guershon	SIBRA, Porto Alegre, Brazil
Susan Heller	ADL, New York
Hadassa Hirschfeld	Israel Information and Documentation Center (CIDI), Holland
Adrian Jmelnizky	DAIA, Argentina
Jeremy Jones	Executive Council of Australian Jewry (ECAJ)
Fanny Kaplan	Comité Central Israelita (CCIU), Uruguay
Sergio Kiernan	Buenos Aires, Argentina
Ruth Klein	B'nai B'rith Canada
Stieg Larsson	*Expo* magazine, Sweden
Wendy Lefko	ADL, New York
Marcos Levy	Comité Representativo de las Entidades Judias de Chile (CREJ), Chile
Pavol Mestan	Museum of Jewish Culture, Bratislava, Slovakia
Middle East Media and Research Institute (MEMRI)	Jerusalem/Washington DC
Monitor	Norway

Luiz Nazário	Universidade de Belo Horizonte, Brazil
Palestinian Media Watch	Jerusalem/New York
Rafal Pankowski	Nigdy Wiecej (Never Again) Association, Warsaw, Poland
Karl Pfeifer	Vienna, Austria
Moise Rahmani	Jewish Board of Deputies, Belgium
Tammy Reiss	ADL, New York
Beatriz de Rittigstein	Centro de Información y Cultura Judaica, Venezuela
David Saks	South African Jewish Board of Deputies
Herbert Schiedel	Dokumentationsarchiv des Österreichischen Widerstandes, DÖW, Vienna, Austria
Brigitte Sion	Coordination Intercommunautaire contre l'Antisémitisme et la Diffamation (CICAD), Switzerland
Laurence Weinbaum	World Jewish Congress, Israel
Michael Whine	Community Security Trust, Board of Deputies of British Jews, UK

The material on the Jewish communities was prepared by the World Jewish Congress Institute.

CONTENTS

Foreword   1

RESEARCH TOPICS
Anti-Jewish Motifs in the Public Debate on Israel:
Sweden – A Case Study
Henrik Bachner   5

Antisemitic Motifs in Belgian Anti-Israel Propaganda
Joel Kotek   26

Al-Aqsa Intifada and 11 September:
Fertile Ground for Arab Antisemitism
Esther Webman   37

The Jedwabne Affair
Robert S. Wistrich   60

BOOK REVIEWS AND PUBLICATIONS RECEIVED   79
Graciela Ben-Dror
Las Derechas: The Extreme Right in Argentina, Brazil and Chile
by Sandra McGee
Joseph Govrin
Antisemitism in Slovak Politics (1989–1999)
by Pavol Mestan
Leonardo Senkman
The Catholic Church and the Jews: Argentina 1933–1945
by Graciela Ben-Dror

GENERAL ANALYSIS
Overview   95
Blaming the Jews:
Antisemitic Images in the Aftermath of 11 September   98

COUNTRY AND REGIONAL ABSTRACTS
Western Europe
   Austria   117
   Belgium   118

Denmark 120
France 121
Germany 123
Greece 125
Italy 126
Netherlands 128
Spain 130
Sweden 131
Switzerland 133
United Kingdom 135

Former Soviet Union and Eastern Europe
Former Soviet Union – Overview 137
Russian Federation 140
Ukraine 142
Hungary 144
Poland 146
Romania 148
Slovakia 150

The Middle East
Arab Countries 152

North America
Canada 154
United States 156

Latin America
Argentina 158
Brazil 160
Chile 162
Mexico 164
Uruguay 166
Venezuela 167

Australia and South Africa
Australia 169
South Africa 171

Appendices 173
Publications of the Institute 183

Foreword

Antisemitism Worldwide provides a forum for academic discussion of various historical aspects of antisemitism and racism in different places and periods, which complements an analysis of these phenomena for the year in review. It is guided by the notion that no coherent examination and understanding of contemporary trends and developments is possible without a thorough acquaintance with the history and manifestations of antisemitism over the centuries.

The present volume is divided into four parts. The first consists of essays on relevant issues (anti-Jewish motifs in the public debate on Israel in Sweden; antisemitic motifs in Belgian anti-Israel propaganda; Arab antisemitism between the al-Aqsa intifada and 11 September; and the Jebwabne affair). The second part consists of book reviews and a list of publications received. The third part is a general analysis of trends for the year in review, with specific focus on "the new antisemitism," as well as an examination of antisemitic images in the aftermath of 11 September.

The last section is a country-by-country survey, divided according to region, since each part of the world has its own characteristic problems in addition to those common to all countries. This survey contains summaries of more detailed reviews which appear on our Internet site (http://www.tau.ac.il/Anti-Semitism/annual-report.html). It provides information on extremist movements, antisemitic activities, attitudes toward the Nazi period and the Holocaust, and the struggle against antisemitism and racism. Countries where there was no evidence of antisemitism in 2001, or where it was not reported, are not included. The surveys present antisemitism in the various countries without delving into their history, and focus only on the situation in 2001 and early 2002. The country/regional review for 2001/2 is supplemented by a series of graphs in the appendices providing statistical data.

Categorization of antisemitic activities sometimes varies from one source to another. Our classification scheme divides these activities into: a) all expressions and modes of propaganda, most notably Holocaust denial, b) violent acts without the use of a weapon, and c) attacks using violent means. It should be emphasized that the survey is based on reported cases only, and that the data presented in the appendices include only violent attacks intended to cause loss of life and cases of actual damage to property. In fact, many more hundreds of minor incidents, such as graffiti, slogans and swastikas painted on walls, and personal insults and harassment, were also registered by Jewish communities and individuals. In many cases, it is difficult to assess whether the injury or damage was motivated by antisemitism, or was an act of hooliganism, since the identity of the perpetrators is often difficult to establish.

It should be noted that the variety of data and materials coming from different areas entails a diversified approach on the part of the authors and editors, thus ruling out complete uniformity in the presentation of the contents, especially with regard to names and references.

Israeli, Jewish and non-Jewish organizations, research institutes and individuals supply the relevant data and material, useful contacts, opinions and assessments, and above all the motivation, for combating antisemitism and racism. Thus, the annual review represents an international effort in this regard. We conclude by expressing our deepest gratitude to all the bodies and individuals who have taken part in this undertaking.

RESEARCH TOPICS

Anti-Jewish Motifs in the Public Debate on Israel
Sweden: A Case Study

Henrik Bachner[*]

INTRODUCTION[1]

Since the outbreak of the second intifada in September 2000 a pattern now familiar in Western political culture has re-emerged: again a more critical stance toward Israel, specifically, of Israeli policies toward the Palestinians, has been accompanied by reports of a rise in antisemitism. Clearly, there has been a marked increase in anti-Jewish incidents in countries such as France. Further – and not least in the case of France – within segments of the Muslim or Arab communities in Europe, antisemitism has become more visible than before. Also, notably, since the UN conference in Durban and the events of 11 September, we have witnessed a revival of both anti-Zionist forms of anti-Jewish propaganda and classical myths of Jewish conspiracies. The center of the current onslaught lies in the Muslim and the Arab world, but some of the ideas propagated have found supporters in the West as well.

It is still too early to estimate the significance of the current wave of antisemitism in comparison to previous waves, such as the one that swept the continent during the 1982 Lebanon War, and which included widespread verbal attacks and stereotyping in the mainstream media. The present situation, however, underlines the need for a better understanding of how antisemitism is related to perceptions of and attitudes toward Israel and the Israeli-Palestinian conflict. The charge, sometimes heard in the public debate but occasionally also in scholarly discussions, that much of the criticism of Israel is influenced by anti-Jewish prejudice, is highly problematic. It is, of course, possible to suspect a deeper animosity behind some of the more unbalanced reporting and comments on Israel, but pointing at bias alone does not adequately substantiate the allegation.

Israel, as has often been stated, is a state whose policies can and should be scrutinized and criticized in the same way as the policies of any other state. Moreover, Israel is a democracy and should be judged by the standards of that political system and its basic values. This means not

---

[*] Henrik Bachner has a Ph.D. from the Department of History of Ideas and Science at Lund University, where he currently works as a research assistant.

5

only that criticism of Israeli policies is legitimate, but also that what might be understood as unfair or exaggerated criticism may be explained in this context.

But what about the frequently repeated charge of double standards – that Israel is judged by different criteria from those applied to other, comparable states? Again, where this can be shown to be the case, it may or may not indicate an attitude influenced by prejudice. More importantly, if not accompanied by specific linguistic expressions, the claim of underlying motifs cannot be analyzed scientifically; hence their existence cannot be satisfactorily demonstrated.

None of this means that anti-Jewish themes within the context of criticism of Israel cannot be identified or assessed. They certainly can, but discerning them requires careful study of the discourse, a precise examination of what was said or written, and an analysis of the ideas, arguments and positions that emerge in a context that comprises the history and tradition of anti-Jewish thinking as well as post-Holocaust and contemporary historical and political realities. By applying this methodology, we can identify myths and stereotypes and elucidate both change and continuity in the antisemitic discourse.[2]

Research indicates that antisemitism in Western political culture since the late 1960s has been intimately connected to, and has emerged within, public debates relating to two central topics: the Holocaust, on the one hand, and Israel and the Middle East conflict, on the other. As the German historian Wolfgang Benz has pointed out, post-Holocaust antisemitism in Europe to a large extent "feeds on feelings of guilt and shame, expresses itself as a denial or trivialization of the Holocaust, and masks itself as criticism of Zionism and hostility toward Israel."[3]

The reality, of course, is not the same in each country. Depending on a number of factors such as historical legacy, wartime experiences and relation to the Holocaust, as well as postwar history and political culture, the depth, intensity, expressions and legitimacy of antisemitism vary greatly between different societies. West European democracies, however, share common features, reflected in the evolution and manifestations of the anti-Jewish discourse during the postwar era. Moreover, while a Holocaust- and guilt-related antisemitism is more evident in countries that were directly involved in the murder of European Jewry, it has gained ground in former allied and neutral countries such as Sweden.

ANTISEMITISM IN POSTWAR SWEDEN

Sweden has a history of anti-Jewish prejudice dating back to the Middle Ages. Christian anti-Judaism contributed to the persistent ban on Jewish immigration, which lasted until 1782, when Jews for the first time were allowed to reside in Sweden without converting to the Christian faith. Their political emancipation was completed in 1870. Although Sweden never experienced a large-scale political antisemitic movement of the kind that emerged in various European countries at the end of the nineteenth century, the modernization of Swedish society strengthened anti-Jewish sentiments among segments of conservative as well as radical and socialist bodies of opinion. In literature, in the comic press, and subsequently also in films, Jews were frequently depicted as racially alien and associated with what many saw as the destructive forces of the new era: capitalism, socialism, urbanization and so forth.

While the extent and strength of antisemitism in late nineteenth century and early twentieth century Sweden remain unclear, recent studies have shown that traditional religious and secular anti-Jewish stereotypes remained an integrated and fairly well-accepted part of Swedish culture until World War II. Negative perceptions of Jews also influenced popular attitudes as well as restrictive government policies toward Jewish refugees from Nazi Germany during the 1930s.[4]

As in many other countries, the impact of the Nazi extermination of Europe's Jews led to strong delegitimization of and a taboo on antisemitism in the dominant political culture of postwar Sweden.[5] While there were occasional outbursts of anti-Jewish rhetoric (as in the case of the assassination of the Swedish UN mediator Count Bernadotte in Israel in September 1948), antisemitism was to a large extent absent from the public debate during the first two decades after World War II. Popular support for Israel was strong throughout this period, yet pro-Israel sentiment also included a tendency to idealize Jews and the Jewish state. This glorification, which stood in sharp contrast to the fairly widespread negative attitudes toward Jewish refugees during the 1930s and the war years, was often accompanied by references to a "bad conscience" or feelings of "guilt" about the Jews.[6]

The Holocaust and the delegitimization of antisemitism did seem to lead to a weakening of anti-Jewish sentiments within the Swedish public, but long-held and deep-rooted prejudices did not totally disappear. An undoubtedly limited yet significant revival could be discerned at the end of the 1960s and the first half of the 1970s, when militant anti-Zionism, propagated by small but influential revolutionary Marxist and radical Christian groups, revitalized some popular stereotypes of Jews.[7]

Although a more critical stance toward Israeli policies and positions in the Arab-Israeli and Palestinian-Israeli conflicts emerged in the public discourse, radical anti-Zionism had little legitimacy at the time. Yet, anti-Zionist arguments, including anti-Jewish components, did slowly influence some circles and intellectuals within the democratic mainstream of Swedish politics, giving these claims a certain measure of respectability and extending the boundaries of speech acceptable in the public arena. In parallel, the taboo on antisemitism seems to have gradually weakened – a trend also observable in the defense of Holocaust revisionism by some well-known Swedish left-wing intellectuals at the beginning of the 1980s.[8]

The effects of these developments could be seen in the reactions to Israel's 1982 Lebanon War, which unleashed marked anti-Jewish reactions in many countries. The scope and intensity of these outbursts seemed to suggest that this antisemitic wave constituted a watershed in the history of postwar European antisemitism. For the first time since World War II, anti-Jewish sentiments on a broad scale had surfaced within the mainstream political culture, not least within the media.[9] Sweden was no exception.

Before discussing the anti-Jewish motifs that emerged in the Swedish public debate on Israel and the Lebanon War, it is important to stress that most of the discussion, which in the main was sharply critical of Israel, cannot be judged as antisemitic. The majority of the articles published – however harsh in condemning the Israeli invasion, its effects on Lebanese and Palestinian civilians, and what was seen as indirect Israeli responsibility for the massacres in Sabra and Shatila – did not contain visible antisemitism. Nevertheless, a significant minority of articles – news reports, editorials, feature articles, readers' letters and political cartoons – did.

Christian Anti-Jewish Themes

An analysis of the Swedish debate elucidates both the persistence and flexibility of anti-Jewish thinking. It shows how stereotypes and beliefs largely absent from the public discourse for decades can be easily revived and adapted to new circumstances. Although Sweden is one of the most secularized countries in Europe, the anti-Israel mood created by the Lebanon War unleashed a flood of age-old Christian anti-Jewish perceptions which were woven into – and rationalized as – criticism of Israeli government policies.

In general, it can be said that the original theological construct of Judaism as the antithesis of Christianity – the contrast between Christian love and forgiveness and Jewish unforgivingness and malevolence – constituted a leitmotif in the antisemitically tainted argumentation during the war. A recurring theme was that of a specific Jewish vengefulness and cruelty, often referred to as an "eye for an eye" mentality, an Old Testament wrath and bloodthirstiness that was said to characterize Israeli behavior.

A columnist in a mainstream paper wrote: "Israel is building its ideology on the Old Testament. We doubt that there can be peace before this unyielding grip has loosened... How different the New Testament is, with its extirpation of differences between Jews and others!"[10] Dozens of readers' letters contained the same reasoning: "Israel's 'holy scriptures', as is well known, are important sources of inspiration when they start their wars of conquest and extermination"; "Now the state [of Israel] has sent its army to Lebanon in an Old Testament fashion."[11] It must be difficult for a Christian, one letter stated, "to quietly accept the acts of violence perpetrated by Jews. How does this correspond to the New Testament and Jesus' message of love?"[12]

These traditional perceptions were also often integrated into a Holocaust- or guilt-related discourse. An editorial in the leading mass-circulation social democratic daily *Aftonbladet* explained the motifs underlying the Israeli invasion in the following way: "Israel is taking a terrible revenge these days, revenge in accordance with the harshest words in the Old Testament, revenge for the horrible suffering that befell the Jewish people in Europe." A few days later the same editorial writer claimed that the Palestinians were being "exterminated" by Israel and that this reminded him of "the persecution of the Jews in Europe."[13]

Other papers followed suit. The conservative *Norrköpings Tidningar* published a letter which, after having claimed that Israel was committing a crime similar to the Holocaust and that "the Jews of today remind one of the likes of Hitler," stated: "It is incomprehensible that Swedish Christians visit Israel as Israel's lust for vengeance has existed ever since World War II."[14]

Grafia, the mouthpiece of the graphic workers union, published – and later, when criticized, defended as legitimate and not anti-Jewish – an analysis of Israel's Lebanon War that claimed: "As for the Israeli bombing of Beirut in the summer of 1982, even this finds support in Judaism... Judaism, then, is a particularly warlike and murderous teaching or 'religion'... Accordingly, the expansionist global and genocidal policy Israel pursues... is totally supported by the holy scripture of Judaism, the Old Testament."[15] These perceptions were also articulated without any reference to religion. The Lebanon War was, as one letter claimed, a result of the Jews' "hunger for power and insatiable lust for revenge."[16]

Another common theme was using the concept of "the chosen people" when criticizing the Israeli invasion. In modern antisemitic thinking the concept of chosenness is often interpreted as signifying Jewish racism – a belief in Jewish racial superiority – as well as purported Jewish striving for power and domination. It is sometimes also used as a code word to enhance traditional ideas of cruelty and bloodthirstiness supposedly embedded in Judaism. All these ideas were manifest in the Swedish press debate on Israel.

The notion of chosenness was frequently suggested as an underlying explanation for Israel's invasion of Lebanon or for the often brutal consequences of Israeli warfare for civilians. One article wondered whether "the legend that they are God's chosen people" was subconscious in their minds while they were pursuing that "cruel war."[17] "Now they are asking for help for the poor victims of the ruthless genocide that 'God's chosen' today are pursuing," another said.[18] Louder protests are needed, a letter claimed, "since 'God's people' are indiscriminately... murdering thousands of defenseless humans."[19] "'God's chosen people' have no right to kill innocent women and children," another writer asserted.[20]

The social democratic daily *Dala-Demokraten* published a letter commenting on the massacre in Sabra and Shatila, which included the following lines: "The Jewish year ended and the new one began with a massacre. Women and children were murdered by 'God's elect nation'. However, the war policy of the Israeli government finds support in the Bible."[21]

The *Grafia* article quoted above explained that according to Judaism "the Jews are God's own people, a specifically chosen people, superior to other peoples." Jewish religion is "racist," the writer continues, "yes, Judaism even orders its chosen people to commit genocide."[22]

The concept of chosenness also figures in anti-Zionist condemnations of the war. "Zionism," one such article claimed, "is a Jewish national movement that aspires for 'God's chosen people' to rule the entire Middle East."[23] The editor of *Proletären*, a communist paper that consistently demanded the elimination of Israel, wrote with reference to Israel's armed forces: "They are God's chosen, with the right to exterminate everything that comes in their way."[24]

The perception of the Lebanon War as the "chosen people's" war was linked to other antisemitic stereotypes, such as the image of the greedy, dishonest and exploitative Jew. The following piece was published under the heading "Moses and Begin" in social democratic *Västgöta-Demokraten*:

> If one believes the old source texts, Israel was God's chosen people. It is therefore perhaps not a difficult choice for such a people, using all the means at its disposal, especially military options, to strive to extend its chosen property and territory...
>
> Jews and pawnbrokers used to be virtually synonymous concepts, but things have moved on and they now invest their assets in the West Bank, which pays a higher dividend...
>
> We need to differentiate between Christianity and Judaism – the Jews follow the law of Moses, a specially composed story, particularly well suited to military and warlike adventures.[25]

In the anti-Jewish discourse the concept of chosenness also merged with the projection of the Holocaust onto Israel or the Jews, with the pursuit of the Lebanon War as a replication of the extermination of Europe's Jews. In the social democratic daily *Arbetet* a well-known writer portrayed the Lebanon War as a Nazi-like genocide rooted in Jewish vengefulness after the Holocaust, as well as in Judaism's idea of chosenness.

> There is a genocide going on in Lebanon. The black-winged shadow of a swastika is being cast over Beirut. Children are being murdered because the Jewish people were persecuted for hundreds of years by the Christians of Europe... Human beings are of no import. Only chosen peoples matter.[26]

In *Arbetarbladet* a columnist complained that the Holocaust "gave Israel a letter of indulgence which has frequently been exploited." Nobody, he claimed, dared criticize Israel for fear of being accused of antisemitism. Now, with Israel's war in Lebanon, the situation is radically different: "One thing is totally clear: The Jews have definitely forfeited their letter of indulgence." The Nazi crimes against the Jews, the article went on, were being repeated by Israel against the Palestinians. There is a great similarity between "Hitler and the Nazis and Begin and the so-called orthodox Jews." The former saw the "Aryan race" as superior to others, while the latter "see themselves as God's chosen people, with special rights in this world." The columnist then gives the following background to the Israeli war in Lebanon:

The Old Testament, still the Holy Scripture to the orthodox Jews, gives advice to Israel on how to treat the enemy. It is recommended that a city which has been conquered should be destroyed. Anything alive should be killed. The enemies of the Jews must be exterminated. These are second-rate people for whom Jehovah has no compassion.[27]

The discourse unleashed – but not caused – by Israel's war illustrates not only the persistence of traditional anti-Jewish perceptions, but also the elasticity and adaptability of these ideas. There were few age-old accusations or beliefs that could not be tailored to the new postwar and post-Holocaust antisemitic discourse. The following passage, which is part of a critique of Israeli policies published in *Östersunds-Posten*, includes the accusation of Christ killing and links the concept of chosenness to stereotypes of Jewish greed and shady business practices as well as to the myth of Jewish political and financial power:

If one calls Israel a democracy, it is a democracy in the spirit of Hitler... The Jews have been busy all over the world, applying their business acumen and lack of scruples in order to acquire influence in the world of finance and exert leverage on policy and presidential elections in America. Because we know the Jews are God's chosen people insofar as, in all periods of history, in all countries, and by every means, they have chosen to steal the property of others. Furthermore, the Jews killed Jesus, which for certain fanatics here at home is such a sacred subject that it gives Israel absolution for all of its foul deeds until the end of time.

The Holocaust related anti-Jewish discourse is influenced by more than the complex problem of guilt. There is also a visible aggressiveness and frustration that seems to stem from the restrictions imposed by the delegitimization of antisemitism. The article quoted above ends with a telling sigh of relief: "The Jews have relinquished for all time the sympathy they received during World War II by utilizing the same methods."[28]

The perception of Israel's Lebanon War as an expression of the "chosen people's" murderousness and "Old Testament" vengefulness attracted many supporters. Other ideas, too, though less frequently used, demonstrated the persistence of the Christian anti-Jewish legacy. The accusation of Christ killing is one such example. This motif was introduced in a more indirect way, in a poem referring to Israeli policies that included the following lines: "Benevolence has been set aside / and

Barabbas[29] remains on the loose."[30] But it was also, as we have seen, used in a direct sense. A letter condemning Israel's war, published by *Västgöta-Demokraten,* assumed that "since the Jews had Jesus crucified, vertical relations... most certainly have become somewhat strained."[31] In another example the writer claims similarities between Israel and "Hitler's Germany," but adds hopefully: "It is not unlikely that the Jews once again will be driven out of Palestine. God's punishment for what they did to his son?"[32]

This motif also entered the anti-Zionist discourse. An anti-Zionist argued in *Smålands Folkblad* that the Israelis were "racists, imperialists and terrorists," and encouraged those defending Israel to recall "who killed Jesus."[33]

Another notion stemming from the medieval anti-Jewish legacy is the association of the Jews with the Devil. Even this motif figured in the Swedish debate on the Lebanon War. A letter-writer in *Folkbladet Östgöten* wondered whether the Jews had "forgotten the Hitler era" and added with reference to present-day Israel that "where Jesus lived, suffered and died, the Devil reigns supreme."[34] Another writer confessed to having "a strong feeling that it is Satan who is giving the orders. Can we not detect the cloven hoof and long tail protruding from under the threadbare cloak of religion?"[35]

In *Aftonbladet* a story resembling the age-old myth of Jewish ritual murder was woven into a comment on the war. In a discussion of the massacres in Sabra and Shatila a foreign correspondent referred to a visit to the Israeli occupied West Bank. At the time, he recalled, a Palestinian child had been found murdered. The perpetrator of this crime was not known, but the correspondent thought he knew what had happened. Singling out Jewish settlers as suspects, he writes: "A child disappeared and was found a few days later in a crevice, shot in the head, ritually executed."[36]

Power, Wealth and Conspiracies

The negative reactions to Israel's Lebanon War served also to reactivate other traditional stereotypes and beliefs. Among them was the myth of Jewish control of world finance, politics and the media, and the conspiratorial fantasies that often accompany such ideas. This mythology was not as prevalent as the images of Old Testament vengefulness and bloodthirstiness, but it did penetrate the debate.

Not surprisingly, ideas of Jewish or "Zionist" control and manipulation of public opinion were strongest in far left anti-Zionist argumentation. They had, after all, been part of radical anti-Zionist propaganda since the late 1960s. The communist paper *Norrskensflamman* supported, in an article, statements made at an anti-Zionist protest rally in Göteborg, which included the claim not only that Zionism was a mirror image of Nazism, but also that Zionism controlled the international media network: "It is lies produced by Zionism that are vomited out through the network of Western media. And the Swedish mass media is taking a very active part in this." An editorial in *Norrskenflamman* a few weeks later added that Zionists shaped Swedish public opinion through their control of much of the media and of publishing houses. The paper referred to "those Zionist forces that are supporting Israel's genocidal policy, for which purpose they have got substantial resources at their disposal: a significant part of the Swedish press, publishing houses and large capital interests. This [influence] makes its mark on television and radio."[37]

Similar motifs emerged in the debate in the mainstream media. A letter in *Västerbottens-Folkblad* claimed that there existed a "a very large and well organized Zionist lobby that exerts much influence on the Swedish press and all other mass media, not least radio and television."[38] An article published in *Nya Norrland* explained that "Jewish organizations and pro-Israeli forces in the world do everything in their power to mislead international opinion about what is happening in Lebanon today." These forces, the article went on, included Swedish Television, the national public service television company, whose re-run of the American series *The Holocaust* in 1982 had the single purpose of "hiding the fact that the victims of inhuman treatment in the 1930s have become the Nazis of our time."[39]

A journalist writing in the liberal *Kvällsposten* and in *Barnen & Vi*, a magazine published by the Save the Children relief organization, considered that "Palestine is a utopia as long as Israel exists." Nothing could threaten Israel. "Israel has the whole of world Jewry behind it, with all its influence and wealth."[40]

In a few cases there were even direct references to the myth of Jewish striving for world domination. In the previously discussed *Grafia* article, the writer concluded that "Judaism aims at cruel world mastery."[41] A letter in the liberal *Göteborgs Tidningen*, which criticized American support for Israel, asked: "Do they [the Americans] believe that they will benefit from future Jewish world domination?"[42]

Although the hostility that surfaced in the media discussion was seldom directed specifically against Swedish Jews, there were a few exceptions. A *Kvällsposten* editorial questioned the loyalty and "Swedishness" of Swedish Jews. "Swedish Jews," the paper wrote, "who blindly support the policy of the Begin government, obviously see the conflict more through Jewish than Swedish eyes." This behavior could backfire on the Jews, the editorial warned, if "the Swedish people" were to reject what Israel was doing. In order to avoid the wrath of the "Swedish people," Jews were advised to express "serious concern" over Israeli policy.[43] In the conservative *Helsingborgs Dagblad* a letter was published in which the image of innate Jewish cruelty was highlighted by references to both the Lebanon War and to kosher slaughter in Sweden. "The Swedish government has given millions of crowns to alleviate the suffering caused by Israel in its latest attack. But there is suffering going on much closer at hand." In Sweden, the letter explains, "every week between three and four hundred chickens are killed, slowly, to satisfy the taste of Swedish Jews."[44]

Liberation Demonology
The analogy between Israel and Nazi Germany in the public debate on the Israeli invasion is a topic that has been touched upon briefly above. This theme deserves additional attention, however, since the projection of Nazism and the Holocaust onto Israel and the Jews is a central element in postwar and present-day anti-Jewish thinking and propaganda. The debate spurred by the Lebanon War indicated that this motif was no longer the preserve of extremist groups, but had gained legitimacy within the mainstream of public opinion.

The characterization of Zionism and Israel as racist and Nazi-like creations had been part of Soviet, Arab and Western anti-Zionist propaganda at least since the end of the 1960s (in the Soviet case it goes back to the German-Israeli rapprochement in the early 1950s). Following the pattern of the Soviet anti-Zionist campaign, Swedish and Western European ultra-left groups had made use of these charges during the 1970s, but at the time they had little, if any, legitimacy within the democratic political culture. Public reactions in 1982 showed this was no longer the case. While it functioned as a catalyst for traditional antisemitism, the Lebanon War also demonstrated that a broader spectrum of public opinion was now willing to accept and reproduce the new anti-Jewish motifs that had developed after and, to a large extent, as a consequence of the Holocaust.

There appear to be several reasons for this change of climate. The increasingly critical view of Israel, no doubt connected to the right-wing nationalist policy of the Begin government, is part of the background. Years of intensive anti-Zionist argumentation might also well have influenced segments of the general public, and although the Marxist new left had almost disappeared from the political scene by the end of the 1970s, some of its ideas continued to surface in the debate on Israel. Yet the problem of coming to terms with the mass murder of European Jews and its historical, political, moral and psychological consequences, seems to have been the major factor behind the increased popularity and usage of images of Nazism and the Holocaust in the debate relating to Israel and its policies *vis-à-vis* the Palestinians. Over time, the taboo surrounding antisemitism also gradually weakened. This increased the level of tolerance for expressions of hostility toward Jews.

These inversions of history have coincided with a historical process in many West European countries where postwar national self-images are being increasingly challenged – a process in which the past relating to the Holocaust is often at the core. These re-examinations and debates are not always welcomed and to some the projection of the past upon the Jews seems increasingly attractive. The new formula – that the Jews are the new Nazis, guilty of a new Holocaust – has relieved guilt feelings and provided a new vehicle for anti-Jewish sentiments to be legitimately expressed.

This, of course, does not imply that all usage of Nazism and the Holocaust as metaphors or analogies in postwar and contemporary political debate should be interpreted in this way. These concepts have become symbols of evil in the postwar world and as such are being used and misused for various reasons – the political discourse in Israel being no exception. To a certain degree, this reservation should also apply to the European debate on Israel. The exploitation of such images in relation to the Jewish state, therefore, might not always be motivated by factors such as those outlined above.

But it is crucially important to acknowledge the fundamental difference between the application of these images to Jews and the Jewish state and the use of Nazism and the Holocaust as metaphors when discussing other topics. Moreover, when these images emerge as a collective mass phenomenon, when significant parts of public opinion in Europe transform the victims of antisemitism, Nazism and the Holocaust into mirror images of their persecutors and murderers – as was the case during the Lebanon War – the complex underlying motives must be taken into account.

Even if the motives behind this type of phenomenon can never be fully explained, there are grounds to support the notion that such expressions are best understood as a form of liberation demonology. The transformation of victim into executioner, of "the Jew" into Nazi, has not only brought relief, but has also given vent to an aggressiveness and frustration which the issue of guilt and the muzzling of expression seem to have generated. This interpretation would appear to be plausible if we look at the argumentation which in many cases supported these representations – the recurring references to "guilt," to irritation over not being permitted to speak in unambiguous terms about Israel and collectivized assertions about the transformation of "the Jews" or "the victims." Moreover, it is given credence by the scope, intensity and, above all, selectivity, in the pattern of association.[45]

The ease with which this imagery is accepted and disseminated, however, is not adequately explained solely in terms of its satisfying emotional needs or – which in part was the case when it was exploited in anti-Zionist argumentation – serving political ends. The portrayal of "the Jew" as a racist, a Nazi and a perpetrator of genocide is also linked to an existing, well-cultivated tradition of reasoning. Since the Middle Ages, Jews have been repeatedly portrayed as symbols of evil. The representation of "the Jew" as a terrestrial incarnation of the Devil has been superseded in the modern era by his depiction as the personification of capitalism and communism. After Auschwitz, absolute evil was represented by racism and Nazism. That the Jews in due time would also be identified with these phenomena, and that parts of the European body of opinion found the linkage plausible, must therefore also be seen against this background. The intimate connection of the new motifs to existing widespread notions is also demonstrated by the fact that they were often supported by and intrinsically interlinked with traditional myths and stereotypes.

An examination of how Swedish media reporting and debate treated and described other conflicts and atrocities that took place at the end of the 1970s and the beginning of the 1980s (for example, the Soviet war in Afghanistan, the Iran-Iraq war, the civil war in Lebanon, the Syrian massacre in the city of Hama and the civil wars in Guatemala and El Salvador) reveals that, they never aroused analogies or images of Nazism and the Holocaust.[46] It seems that it is only when Israel is involved in a war or a conflict that Nazism, the Holocaust, Auschwitz and the Warsaw Ghetto become immediate associations for significant segments of Swedish (or other Western[47]) public opinion. From this we can conclude that it is not the events themselves that unleash these associations, but the identity of one of the involved parties: the Jews. These expressions therefore cannot be satisfactorily explained by reference to the predominant political rhetoric or the factual circumstances of the war. They should rather be understood as primarily an effect of the historical, moral and psychological problems that are a consequence of the

Holocaust, as well as of older, pre-existing patterns of anti-Jewish thinking, nourished by the new Holocaust related resentment. An examination of the Swedish debate during the Lebanon War supports this interpretation.

In July 1982 the communist and anti-Zionist paper *Proletären* noted with great satisfaction: "The accusation that Israel and Zionism use the same cruel methods that Hitler and the Nazis employed against the Jews during World War II is no longer confined to small pro-Palestinian groups – it has become widely accepted."[48] This observation was to a large extent correct.

Within the mainstream press these images quickly became epidemic. With Lebanon as the stage, European World War II history was reshaped with the Jews in the role of Nazi executioners and the Palestinians as Jews being exterminated. That this fantasy had little to do with the war itself, but quite a lot with Europe's and Sweden's troublesome past is also shown by the generalizations that were made. In many articles the writer disclosed not only new insights about Israel, but about Jews in general. "What lessons did the Jews actually learn from Nazism?"[49] "Ought not the Jews to have had enough of heinous acts during the Hitler regime?"[50] "Are they [the Jews] to be allowed to act in any way they like just because they are 'pitied'?"[51] "It surprises me that the Jews have learned nothing from their history."[52] These are all formulations typical of the discourse that emerged.

The way these insights are presented follows a specific pattern. First, there is often a reference to the sufferings of the Jews during the Holocaust; this is followed by the "discovery" that the Lebanon War is a new Holocaust and that the Jews have themselves become Nazi executioners. "Of course we should feel sorry about what the Jews went through in World War II," one article stated. But, it continued, in Lebanon "an extermination is taking place similar to the one the Jews fell victim to during World War II. They are now showing themselves to be the same as the Nazis were then."[53] "Here in Sweden," another writer explained, "we grieved over, and were plagued by, Hitler's mass slaughter of the Jews in World War II. We could never have imagined that the Jews would be the same wild mass murderers as Hitler's simple-minded lackeys."[54] A further example reads: "Without going into the atrocities of the Hitler period in Europe , I felt deep sympathy for the Jews. But now I have changed. Now they are themselves like Hitler… The Jews have become fascists."[55] If many articles of this kind expressed relief, others were outspokenly aggressive: "And forgetful of their own destiny during the Holocaust in Germany, they set to work. And so they commenced their own Holocaust."[56]

This leitmotif appeared in hundreds of editorials, comments, news reports, readers' letters and cartoons. An editorial in *Västgöta-Demokraten* clearly illustrates the central themes behind the new demonology: liberation from frustrating restrictions and/or feelings of guilt. "Throughout the centuries," the paper pointed out, "the Jewish people have suffered horribly and the terrible crimes that were committed against them in Europe during World War II must never be forgotten." But, the editorial continued, the Christian West had been "possessed by its bad conscience" which had led to the fact that nobody dared criticize Israel "for fear of being accused of antisemitism." In the case of the war in Lebanon, however, this apparent barrier seemed to have fallen. "The crimes committed against the European Jews are now being repeated against the Palestinian Muslims," it explained, and went on to suggest that the only just solution to the conflict was "the abolition of the State of Israel in its present form." After the Sabra and Shatila massacre the paper stated that the Israeli army was now identical to "the Nazi special units that acted in Belsen, Auschwitz and Treblinka."[57]

If traditional anti-Jewish themes frequently surfaced in editorials, news reports and other material in the leading social democratic daily *Aftonbladet*, this paper also more systematically than most other publications transformed the Lebanon War into a new Holocaust. On the front page of 17 June 1982, the editor-in-chief declared, under the heading "Genocide": "The State of Israel was created so that we all collectively should atone for a terrible burden of guilt toward the Jewish people." From now on and for months to come every aspect of the Lebanon war would be described in terms associating it with the Nazi genocide of the Jews, the message being instilled through recurring headings such as "The Holocaust" or "The Holocaust in Lebanon."[58]

Aftonbladet's correspondent in Lebanon reported on Palestinians being taken to "concentration camps" and explained that "the [Israeli] extermination of the Palestinian people" was now under way. The well known photo of the Jewish boy guarded by SS troops in the Warsaw Ghetto was placed alongside a photo of Palestinians surrendering to Israeli soldiers in Lebanon. The text accompanying the pictures read: "Nobody forgets the photo from the Warsaw Ghetto in 1943." Today, it continued, "it is the Palestinians that are being exterminated."[59] This message was also frequently repeated in editorial comments. One of them stated: "In Lebanon the Israeli state is staging its own version of the Holocaust."[60] *Aftonbladet* also published numerous readers' letters echoing this motif.[62]

The projection of the Holocaust onto Israel, and onto Jews in general, also gained legitimacy from its usage by leading politicians. Olof Palme, leader of the Social Democratic Party and head of the opposition at the time, referred in a speech to the pain he had felt seeing pictures of "Jewish children in concentration camps and ghettos and realising the terrible crime that had been committed against them." This same pain, he continued, was now felt "when we see pictures of Palestinian children, persecuted in exactly the same way. But this time it is Israel which stands behind [the persecution]."[62] The international secretary of the Social Democratic Party claimed that the war had led to "an extraordinary reversal of roles. Today it is the Palestinians, not the Jews, who are being persecuted and are threatened by 'liquidation'… Today it is the Palestinians who are locked up in a new Warsaw Ghetto."[63]

The notion of the Holocaust being replicated by its victims caught on rapidly. There were hardly any aspects of the Nazi extermination program that were not imitated by the Jewish state. Dozens of articles reported that the Palestinians were forced to wear a sign of recognition similar to the star worn by Jews in Nazi occupied Europe and that Beirut now resembled the Warsaw Ghetto.[64] To a liberal commentator, the Israeli bombardment of Beirut "brought the *Kristallnacht* of autumn 1938 to mind."[65] To the editor-in-chief of *Smålands Folkblad*, the bombing was a terrifying parallel to "the Final Solution."[66] Others described the air raids as an "Israeli 'Lebensraum' massacre."[67] "One hundred Palestinians have been gassed to death," a letter in *Dagbladet Nya Samhället* claimed.[68] The daily *Sydöstran* accused Israel of crimes similar to "the Nazi system of using individuals from what were considered inferior races for medical experiments."[69]

Although Israel was the center of attention, the concepts "Israel" and "the Jews" were, as pointed out, often used synonymously in this discourse. Israel was compelled to repeat the crimes committed against the Jews in Europe, thus revealing the true character of the Jews or what they had become. Israel, then, in this context, functioned as "the collective Jew," both a symbol and an object of projection. This becomes abundantly clear when looking at the way the message was often conveyed: "the victims of inhuman treatment in the 1930s have become the Nazis of our time";[70] "the former victims of the Nazi racist extermination policy have switched roles and have instead become executioners";[71] "the children that 37 years ago were victims of…annihilation, today without any hesitation use the same means against new children";[72] "the Jews of today remind one of the likes of Hitler";[73] "the people that were threatened with extermination by the Nazis… [today] repeat the crimes of their executioners";[74] "the Jews behave in the same way as Hitler and his gang";[75] "it seems as if the Nazi poison was somehow sucked up by the Jews."[76] Having constructed Israel as a Nazi state committing a Holocaust in Lebanon, conclusions were drawn about "the victims of the 1930s," "the former victims," "the Jews" and so forth.

CONCLUSION

The examination of the Swedish public debate on Israel's 1982 Lebanon War elucidates some central characteristics of postwar and contemporary antisemitism. Primarily, it demonstrates the intimate relationship between antisemitism and perceptions, attitudes and reactions to Israel and the Middle East conflict. It indicates that in mainstream political culture the public debate on Israel is a major forum for antisemitism. There appear to be several reasons for this. Two factors, however, are of fundamental importance.

First, as the prime Jewish actor in the global political arena Israel is a focal point for latent antisemitism. The Jewish state – in some cases its sheer existence, but more often its policies and actions – serves as a stimulus for anti-Jewish sentiments and prejudice to become manifest. Israeli policies, especially if seen as provocative, are interpreted by parts of the public through a filter of pre-existing, probably often unconscious, negative stereotypes and beliefs. As was demonstrated during the Lebanon War, Israel, to a substantial number of people, was not a state like other states and did not go to war for motives similar to those of other states. Israel's war became in the eyes of many a "Jewish" war, pursued for specifically "Jewish" motives. Drawing from the reservoir of both Christian and secular anti-Jewish perceptions, the Lebanon War was transformed into a uniquely horrifying war in which "God's chosen people" expressed their "Old Testament" vengefulness and bloodthirstiness as well as their racism, greed and striving for domination. Second, the debate on Israel has been a major forum for antisemitism within mainstream political culture because it constitutes the only public arena where negative attitudes toward Jews can be legitimately articulated, since in this context they can easily be packaged and rationalized as criticism of Israel or Zionism.

Reactions to the Lebanon War, moreover, indicated that the strong anti-Israel mood was accompanied not only by a more visible antisemitism, but also a greater tolerance toward anti-Jewish expressions within the mainstream media. Although antisemitism lacked legitimacy within the democratic political culture, a large number of respected newspapers and periodicals published material that was quite openly antisemitic, and which, under "normal" circumstances, would not have been included. The level of acceptance with regard to antisemitism, then, seems to rise and fall with the fluctuations of public opinion on Israel.

The Swedish debate on Israel's Lebanon War demonstrates the persistence of traditional Christian and secular anti-Jewish myths and stereotypes. Although largely absent from the public discourse for decades, historically- and culturally-rooted images were easily reawakened and formed the kernel of antisemitically tinged argumentation. But the discussion that emerged also demonstrates the adaptability and flexibility of antisemitism as well as the propensity for its renewal. It shows that the consequences of the Holocaust play a crucial role in shaping the features of postwar anti-Jewish thinking and it indicates that the projection of Nazism and the Holocaust onto the Jewish state, or onto Jews in general, constitutes a central element in the contemporary anti-Jewish discourse.

NOTES

1. This essay is to a large extent based on Chapter 6 in Henrik Bachner's study *Återkomsten. Antisemitism i Sverige efter 1945* (Resurgence. Antisemitism in Sweden after 1945) (Stockholm: Natur och Kultur, 1999).

2. The fruitfulness of this approach in analyzing both Israel- and Holocaust-related antisemitism has been demonstrated in a number of studies. See, for example, Micha Brumlik, "Die Angst für dem Vater. Judenfeindliche Tendenzen im Umkreis neuer sozialer Bewegungen," and Hajo Funke, "Bitburg und 'die Macht der Juden'. Zu einem Lehrstück anti-jüdischen Ressentiments in Deutschland/Mai 1985," in Alphons Silbermann & Julius H. Schoeps, eds., *Antisemitismus nach dem Holocaust. Bestandsaufnahme und Erscheinungsformen in deutschsprachigen Ländern* (Köln: Verlag Wissenschaft und Politik, 1986); Lars Rensmann, "Entschädigungspolitik, Erinnerungsabwehr und Motive der sekundären Antisemitismus," in Rolf Surmann, ed., *Das Finkelstein-Alibi. "Holocaust-Industrie" und Tätergesellschaft* (Köln: PapyRossa, 2001); Robert S. Wistrich, *Hitler's Apocalypse: Jews and the Nazi Legacy* (London: Weidenfeld & Nicolson, 1985); Ruth Wodak, Peter Nowak, Johanna Pelikan, Helmut Gruber, Rudolph de Cilla, Richard Mitten, *"Wir sind*

alle unschuldige Täter." *Diskurshistorische Studien zum Nachkriegsantisemitismus* (Frankfurt am Main: Suhrkamp, 1990).

3. Wolfgang Benz, "Tradierte und wiederentdeckte Vorurteile im neuen Europa: Antisemitismus, Fremdenhass; Diskriminierung von Minderheiten," paper presented at the conference *Antisemitismus in Europa*, Berlin, 1992, p. 2.

4. Lars M. Andersson, *En jude är en jude är en jude... Representationer av "juden" i svensk skämtpress 1900–1930* (Lund: Nordic Academic Press, 2000); Steven Koblik, *The Stones Cry Out. Sweden's Response to the Persecution of the Jews. 1933–1945* (New York: Holocaust Library, 1988); Paul A. Levine, *From Indifference to Activism. Swedish Diplomacy and the Holocaust; 1938–1944* (Uppsala: Acta Universitatis Upsaliensis, 1996); Ingvar Svanberg & Mattias Tydén, *Sverige och Förintelsen. Debatt och dokument om Europas judar 1933–1945* (Stockholm: Arena, 1997); Rochelle Wright, *The Visible Wall. Jews and Other Ethnic Outsiders in Swedish Film* (Carbondale/Edwardsville: Southern Illinois University Press, 1998).

5. Antisemitism within the extreme right is not treated in this article. The extreme right continued to openly propagate Jew hatred, but it was marginalized, discredited and isolated and, until recently, had little influence on the public debate.

6. Bachner, *Återkomsten*, pp. 49–150.

7. Ibid., pp. 236–330.

8. Ibid., pp. 354–68.

9. Bernard Wasserstein, *Vanishing Diaspora. The Jews in Europe since 1945* (London: Hamish Hamilton, 1996), pp. 231–2. See also Simon Epstein, "Cyclical Patterns in Antisemitism: The Dynamics of Anti-Jewish Violence in Western Countries since the 1950s," *ACTA*. 2 (1993), pp. 4–6.

10. Texto, *Skövde Nyheter*, 15 June 1982.

11. Andersson, *Västgöta-Demokraten*, 19 June 1982; Tommy Rydén, *Jönköpings-Posten*, 5 July 1982.

12. Undrande, *Östersunds-Posten*, 19 July 1982.

13. Struve/Gunnar Fredriksson, *Aftonbladet* 18 June and 23 June 1982.

14. Förvånad, *Norrköpings Tidningar*, 18 June 1982.

15. Sigvard Casteberg [pseudonym of Christopher Jolin], *Grafia* 20 (1982), p. 9.

16. Lennart Karlsson, *Folket*, 18 June 1982.

17. Magnusson, *Dala-Demokraten*, 1 July 1982.

18. Verner Jönsson, *Nya Norrland*, 8 July 1982.

19. BH, *Sundsvalls Tidning*, 16 June 1982.

20. Broderskap, *Hallands Nyheter*, 24 June 1982.

21. E. van Gelium, *Dala-Demokraten*, 22 Sept. 1982.
22. *Grafia.* 20 (1982), p. 9.
23. Uno Nilsson, *Västerbottens Folkblad*, 30 June 1982.
24. *Proletären* 51 (1982).
25. Emanuel, *Västgöta-Demokraten*, 21 Sept. 1982.
26. Clas Engström, *Arbetet*, 17 June 1982.
27. Vilda Wille, *Arbetarbladet*, 25 Sept. 1982.
28. E.R., *Östersunds-Posten*, 3 Sept. 1982.
29. In the New Testament, a prisoner or criminal mentioned in all four gospels who was chosen by the crowd, over Jesus Christ, to be released by Pontius Pilate in a customary pardon before the feast of Passover.
30. Gumman, *Folkbladet Östgöten*, 22 July 1982.
31. Fredsälskare, *Västgöta-Demokraten*, 12 June 1982.
32. Socialdemokrat, *Värmlands Folkblad*, 31 June 1982.
33. "1926," *Smålands Folkblad*, 2 July 1982.
34. Människovän, *Folkbladet Östgöten*, 18 June 1982.
35. Lapplands ABF:are, *Norrskensflamman*, 10 Aug. 1982.
36. Staffan Heimerson, *Aftonbladet*, 25 Sept. 1982.
37. *Norrskensflamman*, 25 June and 3 Aug. 1982.
38. Östen Karlsson, *Västerbottens Folkblad*, 8 Oct. 1982.
39. Nils Nilsson, *Nya Norrland*, 29 July 1982.
40. Leif Persson, *Kvällsposten*, 19 Sept. 1982 and *Barnen & Vi.* 4 (1982).
41. *Grafia* 20 (1982), p. 9.
42. Ned med vapnen, *Göteborgs Tidningen*, 17 Aug. 1982.
43. *Kvällsposten*, 22 June 1982.
44. AHP, *Helsingborgs Dagblad*, 20 June 1982.
45. See also Wistrich, *Hitler's Apocalypse*, pp. 237–40.
46. Bachner, *Återkomsten*, pp. 416–20.
47. See, for example, Wistrich, *Hitler's Apocalypse*, pp. 238–48.
48. *Proletären.* 48 (1982).
49. Henrik, *Expressen*, 30 June 1982.
50. Walter, *Expressen*, 4 July 1982.
51. Demonstrant, *Kristianstadsbladet*, 14 July 1982.
52. Oscar Agnér, *Dala-Demokraten*, 3 July 1982.
53. PAU, *Aftonbladet*, 27 June 1982.
54. Maria, *Västerbottens Folkblad*, 18 June 1982.
55. Besviken, *Arbetarbladet*, 25 June 1982.
56. Y. Palmgren, *Arbetarbladet*, 27 Aug. 1982.
57. B.A. [Berndt Ahlqvist], *Västgöta-Demokraten*, 24 June and 23 Sept. 1982.
58. Carl-Johan Åberg, *Aftonbladet* 17 June 1982. See, for example, *Aftonbladet*, 4, 5 Aug. 1982.
59. Aino Heimerson, *Aftonbladet*, 16, 17 and 29 June 1982.

60. Lars-Ragnar Forsberg, *Aftonbladet*, 8 July 1982. See also, for example, *Aftonbladet*, 4 Aug. 1982.

61. PAU, *Aftonbladet*, 27 June 1982, Gunilla J., *Aftonbladet*, 10 July 1982, Anders, *Aftonbladet*, 10 July 1982, Verner Jönsson, *Aftonbladet*, 22 Aug. 1982.

62. Olof Palme, speech at the TCO-congress 1 July 1982, published in *Dagbladet Nya Samhället*, 9 July 1982.

63. Pierre Schori, *Stockholms-Tidningen*, 28 July 1982.

64. See, for example, Marianne Lundström, *Västerbottens Folkblad*, 2 July 1982, Axel Gustavsson, *Dala-Demokraten*, 1 July 1982, Cherstin Hansson and Kristina Lindström, *ETC* 1 (1982), p. 29, Sigbert Axelson, *Broderskap*. 39 (1982).

65. Ingrid Segerstedt-Wiberg, *Dagens Nyheter*, 24 Aug. 1982.

66. Y. F., *Smålands Folkblad*, 25 June 1982.

67. Mats Åberg, *Dagbladet Nya Samhället*, 22 June 1982. See also Arne Ljung, *Göteborgs Tidningen*, 18 June 1982.

68. Åke Johansson, *Dagbladet Nya Samhället*, 30 June 1982.

69. *Sydöstran*, 28 Sept. 1982.

70. Nils Nilsson, *Nya Norrland*, 29 July 1982.

71. Socialistiska partiet – Örebro, *Örebro-Kuriren*, 24 June 1982.

72. John Hansen, *Värmlands Folkblad*, 14 June 1982.

73. Förvånad, *Norrköpings Tidningar*, 18 June 1982.

74. Verner Jönsson, *Nya Norrland*, 11 Aug. 1982.

75. Förbannad Malmöbo, *Kvällsposten*, 17 Aug. 1982.

76. Björn Wegerup, *Sundsvalls Tidning*, 29 Sept. 1982.

Antisemitic Motifs in Belgian Anti-Israel Propaganda

Joel Kotek[†]

INTRODUCTION

In early December 2001 the chief rabbi of Brussels, Albert Guigui, was assaulted in the street by a group of youngsters and insulted in Arabic. Surprisingly, perhaps, the attack prompted no expressions of outrage or a wave of solidarity among politicians or in the media, as it might have done had the rabbi been attacked by far right militants. This lack of sympathy may be explained by the fact that the act was perpetrated by immigrants from the Maghreb, themselves potential victims of exclusion and racism, and not by traditional antisemites.

The attack on the chief rabbi was one in a series of anti-Jewish incidents that indicates a clear rise in antisemitism in Belgium. In a press release of 5 December, the Consistoire central israélite de Belgique expressed its "utter horror and concern in the face of such racist and antisemitic acts which, unfortunately, are becoming more and more frequent." Pinpointing the role of the media, it stressed the link between unbalanced attacks on Israel and antisemitic acts: "It is becoming obvious that the hate campaign led by the media... can only encourage this antisemitic violence."

Indeed, since the outbreak of the second intifada articles, commentaries, testimonies and photographs have appeared daily. Israel is portrayed by the Belgian media, notably *Le Soir*, the most widely circulated French-language newspaper in Belgium, as well as by *Vif l'Express*, its weekly supplement, as solely responsible for the violence which has shaken the Middle East for almost two years. Frequently, in their forum pages and in letters to the editor, Israelis are equated with Nazis and in more extreme publications antisemitic motifs appear in anti-Israel propaganda.

It should be noted that focus on the Arab-Israeli conflict in the Belgian public discourse is relatively new. In his study *The Image of the Jews and Judaism in Belgium History Books*,"[1] Maurice Krajzman showed that the destruction of European Jewry and the struggle to establish a Jewish

---

[†] Joel Kotek is professor at the Free University of Brussels, Belgium, and the Ecole Supérieure de Journalisme of Lille; in February 2003 he took up a new post at the Centre d'Etudes Juives Contemporaines de Paris (musée de la Shoah).

homeland were given scant attention in the postwar Belgian press. This lacuna included discussion of the Holocaust itself as well as the question of compensation for survivors. The popular French-language weekly of the postwar period *Pourquoi Pas?,* for example, showed no special interest in the "Jewish-Arab conflict in the Holy Land." Rare articles on the subject that did appear expressed little compassion for the Jews, survivors of the Holocaust. On the other hand, Krajzman notes frequent allusions bordering on the most banal antisemitism.

Between 1945 and 1948, the Belgium political establishment aligned itself with British policy in Palestine, the Jewish national struggle finding support only among Communists. Catholic Belgian society, which was traditionally hostile toward Zionism, expressed open concern about the "return of the Jews to Judea." The Socialist Party's commitment to the Jewish cause was tempered by the ambivalence of its charismatic leader and prime minister Paul-Henri Spaak, an anglophile who feared ruining Belgium's excellent trade relations with the Arab world. During the UN partition vote on Palestine he voted only at the last minute in favor of the plan.

During Israel's war of independence, Jews provided with arms supplies by Eastern bloc countries fought against troops equipped by the West, particularly Belgium. Indeed, in 1948, 49 percent of exports of Fabrique Nationale, the well-known Belgian gunsmiths" went to Arab countries involved in the conflict.[2] However, it would be incorrect to speak of Belgian anti-Zionism at that time; while official Belgian policy toward the Jewish cause might be labeled indifferent or cautious, the majority of Belgian citizens were largely in favor of the Zionist cause.[3]

It was only in the 1980s with the maturing of the New Left (May 1968) ideology and the Lebanon war that the Palestinian cause began to receive attention in the Belgian media and in public opinion, manifested in increasing antagonism toward Israel among various ideological streams. This trend, which came to a head at the beginning of the millennium, was triggered by the outbreak of the second intifada.

One of the chief concerns of Belgian Jews today – and a principal focus of this article – is the fact that criticism of Israel often incorporates negative Jewish stereotypes and antisemitic insinuations, and that supposedly objective criticism of Israel may be rooted in antisemitism. This suspicion, shared by many Jews in Western Europe in particular, was reinforced by events at the UN World Conference against Racism in Durban, September 2001. Denunciation of Israel's policy toward the Palestinians became a pretext for attacking Jews in the Diaspora, who found themselves in the position of being the chief "defendant."

Moreover, so-called anti-Zionist caricatures, which were widely disseminated during the conference, were directly inspired by Nazi illustrations, notably those of *Der Stürmer*.

The aim of this article is to analyze the exploitation of the Holocaust, especially the equation of Israel with Nazi Germany, in anti-Israeli propaganda in Belgium. It will also discuss the usage of classical antisemitic motifs in anti-Israel propaganda and assess the relation between antisemitism and anti-Zionism in the publications of opposing ideological positions.

THE BURDEN OF THE SHOAH – "ISRAELIS AS SUCCESSORS OF THE NAZIS"

The Holocaust era, in contrast to the immediate postwar era, is today no longer considered a taboo subject but an established fact, corroborated by numerous scientific studies, museums, archives, movies and survivors' testimonies. It has been incorporated as an educational and cultural theme in European institutions. Concomitantly, however, there has been a clear tendency in Europe in general and in Belgium in particular to relieve the burden of guilt toward the Jews by equating Israelis with Nazis. In this respect, it is worthwhile noting the words of Simon-Pierre Nothomb, a descendant of one of the leading Catholic families in Belgium, in the daily Brussels-based *Le Soir*:

> How can such a talented and perceptive people as the Jews, who experienced so many atrocities and pain in flesh, blood and spirit, accept today that its government and army inflict upon others who are not guilty of anything, precisely what they suffered themselves? ... The landscape of the West Bank is like a hallucination. Like Poland during its dark years; it is dotted with concentration camps ... The Gaza Strip is an overpopulated prison. You should visit it, you will revise the history of the Warsaw ghetto... As in 1941 Warsaw, the local authorities are ordered to hand over their subjects forthwith, according to lists compiled by the occupying authorities.[4]

Another notable example of the equation between Israel and Nazi Germany was the *Contre-pied* affair. *Contre-pied* is an educational magazine, distributed free-of-charge in 175,000 copies through Democracy or Barbary, a pedagogic think-tank created in 1995 by the Ministry of Education of the francophone Belgian community (Communauté Française Wallonie-Bruxelles) to fight racism and antisemitism. This think-tank, which does irreproachable work on the Shoah, published in

December 2001 a stinging attack on Israel. Accordingly, Israel was solely responsible for the violence that has been tearing the Middle East apart. While not a single word was said on the peace proposals of the Rabin, Peres or Barak governments, the situation of the Palestinians in Gaza was compared to that of the Jews during the Nazi occupation. When the Jewish community learnt of the pamphlet a scandal ensued, leading the minister, President of the Communauté Française Hervé Hasquin, to cancel its contract with the editors of *Contre-pied*. Democracy or Barbary, for its part, simply reiterated that it "had been founded to raise awareness of the Shoah."

The idea of the Jews being capable of committing genocide eases a great many consciences: they have become executioners of the worst kind, like the Nazis. The French philosopher Alain Finkielkraut underlines this trend which may be traced from 1982 onwards. He wrote of those who find joy, shameful joy (*Shadenfreude*) in attacking the Jews through Israel: "What visible relief in the analogies complacently drawn between the Star of David and the swastika, between Beirut and the Warsaw ghetto."

The projection of Israel as a criminal state as a means of alleviating the burden of guilt from World War II is evident in nations where nationalist motives spurred a large part of the local political or religious élite to become Nazi collaborators. This was true of countries such as Croatia and Slovakia, but also of regions such as Flanders. While it is important to underline that there was indeed a "Flanders resistance" (the grandfather of Patrick Dewael, current Flemish prime minister, was a member of the resistance and died in a concentration camp),[5] the phenomenon of collaboration was far more prevalent in the north than in the south of the country. It was in Flanders, and not in Wallonia or in Brussels, that the communal authorities rushed to execute the measures imposed by the occupying forces, and even reinforced them at times.[6] In May 2001, Interior Minister Johan Sauwens, a member of the main Flemish nationalist party Volksunie (VU) was forced to resign after he had participated in a reunion of former Flemish SS men.

Suppression of the past has led to a tendency in certain parts of Flanders to trivialize both collaboration and the Holocaust, and, at the same time, to denounce Israel and particularly its prime minister for crimes against humanity. VU, which has now split in to the VU-ID and Spirit, has traditionally supported an amnesty for Nazi collaborators and opposed Israel. VU members of parliament regularly call for an anti-Israel campaign. On 19 February 2002, during a debate in the federal Chamber of Representatives, VU-ID deputy Ferdy Willems called for a national boycott of Israeli products, because, he alleged, Israel was a racist country.[7]

Another aspect of the linkage between criticism of Israel and antisemitism is the insinuation that the origins of Israel's cruelty and its alleged racism may be found in Judaism. The following text, from the highly popular Flemish *P-Magazine*, illustrates this trend.[8] It contains all the ingredients of the "new antisemitism," and justifies hatred of Jews in the name of human rights and anti-racism.

> I do not like the shape of the country of Israel. To me, its shape is far too thin and far too long. It makes me think of a worm [*tenia*]. I do not like Israel's policies. To me, they are far too bloody and have no respect for the native population. I do not like the Jewish religion in the country of Israel. To me, this religion is too arrogant and parasitic... I am not antisemitic. Palestinians are Semites. Israel is systematically assassinating Semites... Slowly but surely, Europe is liberating itself from the penitence which has been inflicted on it since World War II. Indeed, it is bizarre that it has taken so long for the world to realize that one genocide does not justify another.

Certain Christian circles, too, have taken advantage of the "godsend" that the Israeli-Palestinian conflict represents in their eyes. Their embrace of a profound and ancient opposition to Judaism might explain the *carte blanche* given to *Libre Belgique* on 22 January 2002, when the abbot of Scourmont de Chimay accused Israel of "slow genocide":

> Another dramatic situation is underway. In the course of the last few months, the slow genocide of the Palestinian people has accelerated in an astounding manner. Every attack, the crazy helplessness of a suicide commando against the Israelis becomes the pretext for a massive response.

Attacks on Israel, as these texts demonstrate, provide an outlet for illicit feelings, in the name of progress. To accuse Jews of racism is intentional: once the Jews are considered racists, antisemitism is rid of its racist component and transformed into a doctrine of enlightenment. As the French philosopher Joseph Gabel wrote in 1987: "Anti-racist feelings among the public, which are a healthy reaction to the atrocious horrors of Hitlerite racism, are counteracted by tendencies toward open anti-Zionism, often coupled with unavowed antisemitism."[9]

THE EXTREME LEFT: ANTI-ZIONISM AS A FUNCTION OF
ANTI-AMERICANISM AND ANTI-CAPITALISM

In his study on the almost Manichaean attitude of the extreme left in Western Europe toward Israel, Pierre-André Taguieff uses the term judeophobia, coined by Pinsker. According to Taguieff, Israel is perceived not like other states, but as the epitome of evil without which the world would be far better off. This approach may be found in the publications of almost all leftist ideological trends and groups, such as the neo-Christian humanitarian movements, a large proportion of the "new anti-imperialists" and other neo-anti-globalization groups, as well as amongst "anarcho-Trotskyists," pacifists and Communists. Old rhetoric such as "anti-racist," "anti-imperialist" and "anti-fascist" is being revived to enable the construction of an utterly diabolical figure, a composite of Satan: the United States/Israel/ the Western world.

> One can observe a new, grand, populist vision of worldwide expansion: the "rich" baddies against the "poor" goodies. From this one can conclude that the enemies of the "Zionists" are simultaneously the enemies of the "Americans," and that these enemies are merely "victims," who are in a state of legitimate revolt. Islamism is the anti-capitalism of the enlightened, who have been metamorphosed into fanatics due to their resentment against the West (a category which includes the Zionist entity). The stereotype of the "rich Jew" is therefore recycled, causing one to overlook plutocratic circles, which, particularly in the Arab-Muslim world, finance the Islamist networks and terrorist organizations.[10]

Indeed, antisemitic stereotypes such as the avaricious Jew, and the capitalist and the corrupt Jew are barely disguised in the anti-Israel propaganda of the extreme left. The concept of a world Jewish conspiracy appears as American-Israeli imperialism or Zionist imperialism. A linkage is made between America, Israel and "globalizing" capitalism.

The speech made by Belgian humanitarian guru Pierre Galand, president of the Forum des Peuples, member of the Belgian sector of the Amis du Monde Diplomatique of the Belgo-Palestinian Association and professor of the Free University of Brussels, illustrates this attitude. The text, which was used in propaganda attacks against Israel in Durban, was disseminated through the website of the Maoist Parti du Travail de Belgique (Workers Party of Belgium). By relating to the evils of capitalism alongside Israel's alleged deeds, an inevitable link is created based on leftist stereotypes:

The historical dialogue organized by the UN on racism has turned into a confrontational and door-slamming event, because the North officially refutes what is evident: Blacks, Indians and so many "minorities" are still suffering the agonies of colonialism... Never have the rich of the North agreed to provide the 1 percent of their GDP for the development of the South... Never has there been an honest settling of the rates of raw materials of Southern provenance. In this context... Palestine has become the new Vietnam, the symbol of the unjust war. A people deprived of its rights, just like the Vietnamese of 50 years ago, the Palestinians represent in the eyes of a growing number of peoples, citizens movements, youth and the resistant South, a heroic people, who defend their basis rights and above all their dignity, in the face of an aggressive Israel which the West fails to firmly condemn.[11]

With Israel and capitalism subtly equated in evil, the myth of the capitalistic Jew, the icon of French nineteenth century antisemitism, is resurrected. The roots of this antisemitic attitude may be found in the writings of the utopian Socialist Charles Fourier and of Alphonse Toussenel, author of *The Jews, Kings of Our Times*: "I define the name of the despised Jew, any type of trafficker, any non-productive parasite,who lives from somebody else's substance and work."[12]

The ritual murder myth – the allegation that the Jews killed innocent Christian children – has also penetrated anti-Zionist propaganda. One of the oldest antisemitic allegations, it brought about the destruction of many Jewish communities; even after World War II this accusation led to the pogrom in Kielce, Poland, in 1946. Lately, this myth, which originated in the Christian word, has been transplanted to the Arab world where it is exploited in the context of the Israeli-Arab conflict (see www.tau.ac.il/Anti-Semitism/asw2001-2/arab.htm). A version of the myth disseminated by the Palestinians is the accusation of organ theft. On 24 December 2001, a date that is undoubtedly not accidental, the official paper of the Palestinian Authority accused the Israelis of using Palestinian body parts "Clear signs indicate that the occupying authorities steal parts of martyrs' corpses during the time they hold them, so that they can use them in Israeli hospitals, particularly for Israeli patients who need transplants."[13] On 16 January 2002, "photographs," allegedly of the dissected corpses of three children, were disseminated via the Internet. Although clearly rigged and unverified, the information was immediately relayed by the majority of sections of the main anti-globalization press agency Indymedi, including on 17 January, Indymedia

Belgium, which is particularly prone to primitive antisemitic attacks. The agency's comment bore a religious overtone: "If this is true, then may God bless Israel."

CONCLUSION: ANTI-ZIONISM AS A CULTURAL CODE

Belgium has not, in the course of several months, become an antisemitic country that must be denounced to the rest of the world. The Jews in Belgium do not suffer discrimination. It is, however, a matter of concern for them to observe a real rise in antisemitism in the country.

As demonstrated above, antisemitism emanates both from Catholic circles and the extreme left, as well as from a large segment of the extreme right. These sectors have taken advantage of the Israeli-Palestinian conflict to release the antisemitic world from its longstanding burden of guilt of the Shoah, which not only seems to have lost its power to curb antisemitic passions, but actually appears to intensify them. "For the European progressives," stresses Alain Finkielkraut, "we are the dregs of the earth ... They equate the Jewish State with a Nazi state. For them, we [the Jews] cannot defend a Nazi state, unless we are ourselves are Nazis, and we cannot criticize certain Palestinian politicians from a perspective of peace... To summarize: 'the swastika, is our next yellow star'."[14]

The temptation to disguise the emotional charge of judeocide with radical criticism of Israel is becoming more and more explicit, both on the right and the left. It seems that today anti-Zionism is, unconsciously for many, a means of extirpating a sense of guilt toward the Jews, who were treated so barbarously. Compensating for their own cowardice and the less than exemplary behavior of their parents and grandparents during the war, some of them have adopted an ostensibly responsible and determined position in favour of today's supposed victims of injustice and contemporary barbarity. These victims are almost exclusively the Palestinians, while the rest of the world's outcasts, victims of gross inequalities, of colonial, ethnic and fratricidal wars, and of genocide, receive scant attention.

Another type of antisemitism has emerged in Belgium as well, from a sector that is most vulnerable to xenophobia: the population of Maghreb origin. Since the second intifada, some intellectuals have minimized this phenomenon on the pretext that it is linked to developments in the Middle East conflict. They may not be wrong: once a state of Palestine is created, the current resentment toward Jews of a large proportion of youth of Maghreb origin may indeed fade. However, when a generation of young Muslims has been raised to hate Jews, will the image of the Jew child-killer and the Jew blood-sucker magically disappear? The recent attacks against places of worship in Brussels and elsewhere in Europe demonstrate the influence of virulent antisemitic propaganda that has been circulating among Arab-Muslim circles.

Another theory that might explain the intensity of anti-Israeli hatred is the search for a scapegoat – a role imposed upon the Jews since the Middle Ages. Zionism is today described both by the extreme right and the extreme left, as well as by champions of human rights, as one of the evils of the world, and as such is offered as a scapegoat.

The capacity to identify the scapegoat is, according to René Girard, one of the primordial components of Western culture. The French philosopher showed in *La violence et le sacré*[15] that the search for a scapegoat serves as a universal mechanism of conflict resolution. It is possible to discern a recurring theme in myths throughout the world: the murder or expulsion of an individual – maybe a god or a hero, a marginal figure or a monster – who has aroused the collective violence of the community. The disappearance of this figure will restore peace to the community.

Scorned by Christians and Muslims alike, Judaism is nevertheless sacred in their eyes because it represents the source, without which neither one nor the other would exist. Since neither Christianity nor Islam can explain itself without Judaism, this leads to an ambiguous relationship with the Jews, whom they regard both as a people of God and a traitor to His message, and in Christianity, even killers of the Messiah. Sanctified, despised and envied at one and the same time, it is hardly surprising that since the Middle Ages the Jewish people has been targeted as a scapegoat. In the nineteenth century socialists thinkers such as Marx and Proudhon attacked the "Jew of finance." Kautsky, who perceived antisemitism as a form of social contest, went so far as to salute antisemitic movements in Hungary, which, according to him, "will go beyond its focus in order to reach in the long run, not only the Jews but all of the possessed."[16] Judeophobic anti-Zionism therefore appears as a sort of metaphor for anti-capitalism. It is within this context that we should understand the hatred of Baader-Meinhof member Ulrika Meinhof, who said: "Auschwitz meant that six million Jews were killed and thrown on the furnaces of Europe for what they were: Jews of money."[17] In his time, August Bebel denounced this form of socialism as the "socialism of the idiots."[18]

Today, with Israel in the tailor-made role of the scapegoat, the guilty party, it has even been suggested that it might be sacrificed once and for all for the sake of peace and quiet. As Pierre Taguieff stated:

If Israel did not exist, peace and justice would rule in the Middle East. This leads to a subsidiary argument, namely, as a result of this non-existence Islamic terrorism could no longer justify itself or have any reason to exist – which presupposes that today it does have a reason! The practical and programmatic conclusion of such argumentation can thus be explained: Israel is one country too many and must disappear.[19]

In countries such as Belgium, with its inglorious colonial past and its present incessant criminal scandals (the Killers of Brabant,[20] the Cools[21] and the Dutroux Affairs,[22] to name but a few), Israel or Zionism can play a significant role. They can expiate once and for all Europe's crimes and its colonial and imperialistic past

Thus, from Brussels to Paris and from London to Copenhagen, the concern that is sweeping the Jewish communities is less about criticism of Israel than about the extremely negative images and strong insinuations that have resulted from it. European anti-Judaism has found an unexpected and surprising reinforcement in the antisemitism borrowed by Arab/Muslim nations, which have amplified it and rendered it contemporary. The antisemitism of the Arab and Muslim world is a confused mixture of Christian myths, medieval accusations, Nazi images, and revisionist and Islamist fables. Its rebound to the very heart of the West, which was thought to have eliminated such phenomenon, constitutes a sinister threat.

NOTES

1. Maurice Krajzman, *The Image of the Jews and Judaism in Belgium History Books* (Centre National des Hautes Etudes Juives, Bruxelles, ULB, 1973).
2. Catherine Berny, *La terre trop promise, la Belgique et Israël, 1947–1950* (Louvain, 1988), p. 121.
3. The Jewish cause was more popular within the French speaking part of Belgium, which was more secularized than the Flemish part. The majority of socialists, liberals and communists were in favor of a Jewish state. The Catholics were more cautious, if not hostile.
4. "L'ordre va-t-il régner à Gaza?" *Le Soir*, 18 Dec. 2001.
5. See his book *Respect mutuel*, (Brussels, 2002).
6. Lieven Saerens, *Vreemdelingen in een wereldstad. Een geschiedenis van Antwerpen en zijn joodse bevolking (1990–1944)* (Tielt, 2000).

7. Chambre de Représentants de Belgique, 19 Feb. 2002, Ref. Doc. 50 0025/305.

8. *P-Magazine* 49 (7–13 Dec. 2001).

9. Joseph Gabel, *Réflexion sur l'avenir des Juifs* (Paris: Méridiens Klincksieck, 1987), p. 67.

10. Pierre-André Taguieff, *La nouvelle judéophobie* (Paris, 2001), p. 23.

11. "Réflexion à propos de Durban, www.ptb.be/international/article.phtml?section=AIAAABBV&object_id=5976, 6 Sept. 2001.

12. Alphonse Toussenel, *Les Juifs, Rois de l'époque. Histoire de la féodalité financière* (Paris, 1847), p. 83.

13. http://belgium.indymedia.org/front.php3?article_id=15904 &group=webcast.

14. "Une croix gammée à la place de l'étoile," chronique d'Alain Finkielkraut, *L'Arche* 531–2, (May–June 2002).

15. René Girard, La violence et le sacré (Paris, 1998).

16. Gabel, *Réflexion sur l'avenir des Juifs*, p. 67.

17. Henri Arvon, *Les Juifs et l'idéologie* (Paris, 1978), p. 52.

18. See Robert Wistrich, *Socialism and the Jews: The Dilemmas of Assimilation in Germany and Austria-Hungary* (Littman Library of Jewish Civilization series, 1982).

19. Taguieff, *La nouvelle judéophobie*, p. 54.

20. Unsolved series of brutal murders committed in the 1980s in the Brabant region.

21. Assassination of a former deputy prime minister and respected socialist leader in 1991.

22. 1995 kidnapping and murder of young girl by pedophile.

Al-Aqsa Intifada and 11 September:
Fertile Ground for Arab Antisemitism

Esther Webman‡

INTRODUCTION

Arab Islamic antisemitism was given a further boost by the continuing intifada, which erupted in September 2000, and by the September 11 attacks on the US. This essay examines the impact of these two events on the antisemitic discourse in the Arab world and on the rationalization of hatred and animosity toward Israel and Jews at large. It establishes that the trend of radicalization, discerned following the outbreak of the intifada (see *ASW 2000/1*), not only continued but intensified as a result of an international event ostensibly not directly linked to the Palestinian-Israeli conflict.

This radicalization was manifested in several ways:

-crude attacks – intertwined with antisemitic allusions – on the newly elected prime minister of Israel Ariel Sharon (February 2001);

-popularization of antisemitic motifs, such as the blood libel and the Jewish conspiracy to control the world;

-equating Zionism with racism and Nazism in the struggle against Israel in international forums;

-embracing Holocaust denial as a means of delegitimizing Israel and Zionism;

-sanctioning suicide attacks against Israeli civilian targets as well as attacks on Jewish targets worldwide.

The sanctioning of suicide attacks and the equation of Zionism with racism are intended to delegitimize not only the occupation of the West Bank by Israel, but Israel's right to exist, while resorting to the ancient motifs of the blood libel and the Jewish conspiracy to control the world is an attempt to delegitimize the Jewish people as a whole. The media has become a powerful tool in shaping the collective consciousness, exacerbating the conflict "through the projection of victimization, false statements, justification of violent actions and demonization of the 'other'."[1] At the beginning of June 2001, there was a short respite in

---

‡ Esther Webman is a researcher at the Stephen Roth Institute and the Dayan Center, Tel Aviv University.

Palestinian media incitement due to the prospect of a negotiated cease-fire,[2] but it was revived with the escalation in violence.

RADICALIZATION OF ATTITUDES AND DISCOURSE

The al-Aqsa intifada, which entered its second year in 2001, united nationalist and Islamist forces, creating a dynamic of change in the domestic Palestinian balance of power in favor of the Islamists; this, in turn, led to radicalization of the street and of the discourse against Israel. According to surveys conducted by Khalil Shikaki, director of the Palestinian Center for Policy and Survey Research, for the first time since 1995 the intifada brought about a significant shift of loyalty from the nationalists to the Islamists. By July, the Islamists had increased their support by 60 percent, rising to 27 percent. Moreover, Shikaki predicted that within a few years they would become "the mainstream with a majority of the Palestinian street supporting them."[3] Although the intifada had reached an impasse even before the September 11 events, 80 percent of Palestinians supported its continuation in April, despite the suffering and destruction inflicted on them, and over 70 percent supported suicide attacks (see also below).[4] Calls to impose an embargo on Israeli products and sever any normalization ties were voiced by the Palestinians. At the beginning of February Israeli produce was burnt in the center of Ramallah by activists of the Popular Committee for the Boycott of Israeli Produce.[5]

A similar trend of radicalization typified the general mood in the rest of the Arab world. Popular sympathy with the Palestinians, prompted by reports of the effects of Israeli military escalation in response to the violence, exerted strong pressure on Arab governments to undertake a more aggressive stand toward Israel, but they continued to combine belligerent rhetoric with practical self-restraint. The Jordanian authorities banned anti-Israel demonstrations, but could not prevent the activities of the powerful anti-normalization organizations, which have been engaged in a witch-hunt of Jordanians with links to Israel.[6] This gap between popular sentiment and government behavior was manifested also in the reactions to the September 11 events (see below).

A conference in support of the intifada was convened on 23-25 April in Tehran, bringing together about 500 representatives from Arab and Muslim countries. The conference, which opened with a harsh attack on Israel and Zionism by Iranian president 'Ali Khamene'i, adopted a final communiqué calling for the continuation of the intifada as the only option in the struggle against Israel.. The conference, together with the highlighting of Hizballah's experience in the liberation of South Lebanon as a model for the Palestinians, was part of a deliberate attempt by Iran and Hizballah to increase their involvement in the Palestinian-Israeli conflict and boost support for radical elements such as Hamas and Islamic Jihad. A similar conference had been held in Tehran in support of the first Palestinian intifada in October 1991.[7]

Egyptian expert on Jewish studies 'Abd al-Wahhab al-Masiri concluded that if the Palestinians managed to sustain the intifada, this would signal "the beginning of the end of the Zionist entity." This end was determined not only due to its colonialist nature, but because the Zionist entity could neither defend itself nor secure the interests of the West, its traditional supporter, which could hardly guarantee its own security.[8] Hizballah leader Shaykh Hasan Nasrallah ended his speech at the Tehran conference in April with a fiery warning: "Zionists can get their luggage and go back to wherever they came from."[9] In a Friday sermon on 21 September, Shaykh Muhammad Ibrahim al-Madhi predicted that the war between Arabs and Jews would continue to escalate "until we vanquish the Jews and enter Jerusalem as conquerors … heralding an Islamic caliphate with Jerusalem as its capital."[10] Al-Madhi, a PA official, reflects in his statements the extremist Islamist view, which represents the Jews as a threat to the entire world and the conflict as an irreconcilable struggle between Muslims and Jews.[11] Hamas believes that the worse the situation gets, the quicker "salvation" will come. The solution to the problem "is the sum total of the jihad of the Palestinian people," said Hamas political leader Shaykh Jamal Mansur in an interview.[12] London-based Islamist Azzam Tamimi also foresaw the demise of the Jewish state in an interview to an Israeli magazine. However, he welcomed any Jew who wanted to stay in the Muslim entity that would be established.[13] Al-Madhi, in another Friday sermon in Gaza, broadcast live on PA [Palestinian Authority] TV in June expressed a similar view.[14] Acceptance of the Jews as *ahl al-dhimma* (religious minority) under Muslim rule, the status that prevailed from the seventh till the early 20th century, was a prominent issue in the Arab argumentation against the State of Israel. It was also specified in the covenants of the PLO and Hamas, to prove that they differentiated between Jews and Israelis and Zionists and that Muslims were traditionally tolerant toward the Jews.

Antisemitic Allusions in Attacks on Israel's Prime Minister

Arabs greeted Sharon's election victory in February with a mixture of fear, revulsion and dismay. The mere fact that he was elected was seen as proof of Israel's belligerent and terrorist nature.[15] Criticism of Israel's retaliatory policies in the West Bank and the Gaza Strip turned into personal attacks on Sharon the man, and the acts associated with him, such as the October 1953 Qibya affair (in which innocent Palestinians civilians were killed by Israeli soldiers) or the September 1982 Sabra and Shatilla massacre (perpetrated by Christian militia men in these Palestinian refugee camps). The Arab press was unanimous in portraying Sharon as driven by hatred for the Arabs and a lust to exterminate them.[16] Egyptian journalist Wajih Abu Zikra wrote that Sharon considered the Palestinians to be inhuman, "dogs that should be exterminated." Sharon, he went on, had dreamed about their extermination since the 1960s, and planned to continue the ethnic cleansing policies of former colonial states. Further, Abu Zikra compared Sharon's attempts to create a negative image of the Palestinians to Goebbels' propaganda against the Jews. However, Sharon's cruelty toward the Palestinians far outweighed Hitler's treatment of the Jews; moreover, in contrast to the "so-called" Holocaust which was only a "myth," Sharon actually planned to exterminate the Palestinians.[17]

Arab writers seemed to be competing for metaphors in which to depict Sharon's alleged propensity for killing. "Bloodthirsty butcher,"[18] "diabolical murderer,"[19] "damned dog," and "snake head,"[20] "a new Hitler who surpasses the Nazi leader,"[21] "Israel's Milosevic"[22] and "war criminal,"[23] were common ones. Egyptian editor Muhammad Salmawi criticized Western hypocrisy for accepting Sharon while rejecting Austria extreme right leader Jörg Haider.[24] According to the Islamic Jihad mouthpiece al-Istiqlal (24 May), Islamist guru Shaykh Yusuf Qardawi even ruled that a Muslim who shook Sharon's hand should wash his own hands seventy times.

The media attacks on Israel's prime minister were accompanied by calls for Arab governments to unify their position in order to confront Sharon's threats and bring him, together with other "Israeli war criminals" to justice in the proposed international war crimes tribunal.[25] Arab lawyers associations discussed the preparation of files on "Zionist crimes" against Arabs to be used in future trials. In Lebanon the legal aspects of demanding compensation from Israel were also discussed, especially the possibility that such claims might be interpreted as recognition of the "Zionist entity." [26] These calls converged with the actual submission of a demand in June to the Belgian appeals court to prosecute Sharon, by the Arab-European League in Belgium, representing Palestinian survivors of the Sabra and Shatila massacre.[27]

Popularization of Antisemitic Motifs

Variations of three classical antisemitic motifs – the poisoning of wells, the blood libel and the Jewish conspiracy described in *The Protocols of the Elders of Zion* – emerged in the Arab anti-Israeli discourse. Israel was also accused of pursuing a systematic racist extermination policy.[28] Jordan's Islamist weekly *al-Liwa'* reviewed a new book by 'Ali Sa'ada, entitled *al-hulucust al-filastini. tarikh al-'unf al-filastini... al-ibada al-jima'iya* (The Palestinian Holocaust: History of Aggression against the Palestinians... Collective Annihilation) (27 June). Based on reports published in Palestinian as well as other Arab papers, the book claimed that Israel had been using depleted uranium and nerve gas in its aerial raids on Palestinian territories and south Lebanon. Palestinian representative to the UN Nasir al-Qidwa even demanded, in a memorandum to the Security Council at the end of January, that an international team be set up to investigate the Palestinian allegations. Chairman Yasir 'Arafat made a similar allegation at the Davos economic summit on 28 January.[29] The Syrian daily *Tishrin* charged that Israel was intentionally polluting the waters of the Mediterranean Sea with chemicals and poisonous gases,[30] turning the Palestinian people into victims of a holocaust.[31] *Al-Liwa'* (2 May) repeated the allegation (see *ASW 1999/2000* and *2000/1*) that Israel had contaminated Palestinian water sources. The PA, for its part, claimed that Israel had dropped poisoned candies from planes in order to harm Palestinian children.[32]

Syrian President Bashar al-Asad also made antisemitic remarks. During the visit of Pakistani President Pervez Musharraf in January, he declared that Israel had been "a state based on loathsome racist values" since its inception by a bunch of "racist gangs."[33] At the Arab summit held in Amman in March he claimed that Israeli public opinion was more racist than Nazism,[34] a view he reiterated on his visit to Spain in early May.[35] His remarks at a ceremony welcoming Pope John Paul II on 5 May provoked the strongest reaction. In an effort to solicit the pope's sympathy and support for the Palestinian cause, he attacked Israeli "brute policies" in Palestine and the Golan Heights. Seeking historical precedents that would emphasize common denominators between Muslims and Christians, he raised the centuries-old specter of the blood libel of Jews as Christ-killers – those, he said, "who try to kill the principles of all religions with the same mentality with which they betrayed and tortured Jesus Christ" and made similar attempts on Muhammad. The portrayal of the Jews as the natural enemy of Christianity is not new in Arab rhetoric, having been manifested in Arab reaction to Christian-Jewish rapprochement since the second ecumenical council in 1965. In response to the international uproar his remarks aroused, Asad noted that no one could accuse the Semite Arabs of being antisemites,[36] while Syrian columnists accused the Western media of leading a campaign to distort Syria's image before and after the pope's visit. They also charged international Zionism with waving the sword of antisemitism against anyone who dared expose the truth about Zionism and Israel.[37] Syrian historians even maintained that Pope John Paul II was "the architect of a conspiracy to undermine the Catholic Church by placing it under the control of the Jews."[38]

Frequent references were made to *The Protocols of the Elders of Zion*. Articles emphasizing the importance of psychological warfare in the psyche of the "Hebrew state," cited them to prove the Jews' premeditated plan to control the international media and manipulate world public opinion.[39] More disturbing, perhaps, was the new trend of incorporating antisemitic themes into the arts, thus popularizing them among large segments of the population. For example, a 30-part series documentary called *Horseman without a Horse*, based on the false *Protocols* was broadcast in Egypt.[40]

Abu Dhabi satellite TV, one of the most popular channels in the Arab world, broadcast a series during the month of Ramadan entitled "Terror Affairs," which included a satirical sketch on the Jewish blood libel. The actor who played Israeli Prime Minister Ariel Sharon feasted on a bottle full of red liquid, which he gleefully explained to a young man with a skullcap and side-curls, was the blood of Palestinian children. In another scene he confessed that for his twentieth birthday he had asked to slaughter twenty Arab children and "drink their blood." A third showed Dracula, the mythical cold-blooded vampire, about to sink his teeth into Sharon's neck, only to be reported dead, poisoned by Sharon's "filthy blood."[41]

The growing sympathy for the Palestinian cause led Egyptian as well as Syrian and Jordanian film and theater producers to promote the Arab-Israeli conflict as a major subject in their works.[42] One of four new films contemplated in Egypt is an adaptation by Egyptian producer Munir Radhi of Syrian Defense Minister Mustafa Tlas's book *Matzah of Zion*. One of the political goals of the project, Radhi explained, was "to provide a response to the many Zionist films distributed by the American film industry and supported by the Zionist propaganda apparatus, among them *Schindler's List*, which defends the idea of the Jews' right to Palestine." The film will be based on the story of Father Toma, allegedly slain in 1840 by the Jew David Harari, and will expose "Harari's hit list" of prominent personalities, as well as the link between

Western imperialism and the Zionist movement.[43] The last scene in the life of Father Toma was also produced as a tele-drama.[44] Another film, *Friends or Business*, featuring a suicide bomber, was screened in August in Cairo. According to Philip Smucker of the *Christian Science Monitor* (*CSM*), "the movie was the boldest of several popular theater and movie productions... focus on the bloodshed in Israel." It aroused fears among Western diplomats that it might incite further radicalism and imitation.[45]

Palestinians at al-Najah University in Nablus marked the first anniversary of the intifada by opening an exhibition on 23 September which re-enacted the August 19 terrorist attack in Jerusalem, in which a suicide bomber killed 15 Israelis at a Sbarro pizza restaurant. The exhibition was organized by student supporters of Hamas. Visitors trampled on Israeli and US flags to enter a room where body parts and pizza slices were strewn around. The exhibit included a large rock in front of an effigy of a religious Jew. A recording from inside the rock repeated the common *hadith* (oral tradition): "Oh believer, there is a Jew hiding behind me, come and kill him".[46]

The UN Conference against Racism in Durban

Equating Zionism with racism and Nazism is not a new motif in the Arab antisemitic discourse. In 1994 the revoking of UN resolution 3379 (1975), which equated Zionism with racism, was met with strong Arab protests. However, the new crisis in Israeli-Palestinian relations, which adversely affected Israel's foreign relations, seemed to converge with Arab/Muslim assertiveness and to encourage blatant utilization of this motif in the struggle against Israel in international forums. From early 2001 Arab representatives were reportedly trying to revive UN resolution 3379.[47] By March about one thousand Arab intellectuals of all political stripes had signed a petition to this effect.[48] A similar call was issued by 'Ali 'Aqla 'Arsan, president of the Syrian Arab Writers Association, who also suggested establishing a documentation center for Zionist crimes and carrying out studies on the relations between Nazis and Zionists.[49] In mid-July, the fourth "Arab regional conference against racism," was held in Cairo with the participation of about 70 Arab and international human rights organizations. The conference, which convened under the slogan "together we'll put an end to the last racist regime," dealt extensively with "Israeli racism," and called for the establishment of a special international court for trying "Israeli war criminals. Among the European participants was the Belgian lawyer Luc Walleyn, representing the Palestinians in the possible case against Sharon.[50] The main goal of an association for the struggle against racism formed in Egypt in August was defined as crystallizing an Arab cultural and intellectual response to the Zionist project. The association sent an open message to the Durban conference urging it to adopt the notion that Zionism is a form of racism.[51]

Indeed, the culmination of these Arab and Muslim efforts were their activities at the World Conference against Racism, Racial Discrimination, Xenophobia and Related Intolerance, which convened in Durban, South Africa (see *General Analysis*) at the beginning of September. Encouraged by the declaration of the International Conference of Non-Governmental Organizations Defending Palestinian Rights adopted in Tehran on 23 April,[52] Arab and Muslim delegations sought to turn the Durban conference into an international tribunal against Zionism and Israel. Hence, they attempted to expunge references to antisemitism, trivialize the Holocaust, and above all, reintroduce the equation between Zionism and racism into the conference resolutions. The Arab media supported these attempts by publishing countless articles stressing "Zionist crimes" against the Palestinian people and the Arabs.[53] In keeping with Syria's traditional emphasis on this equation (see *ASW 2000/1*), Foreign Minister Faruq al-Shar'a, in his speech at the conference, described Israel as "the last racist bastion" and the Syrian delegation made a last-ditch attempt to indirectly brand Israel as a racist state in the final conference declaration.[54]

The American walkout from the conference was denounced by Arab League Secretary, former Egyptian Foreign Minister 'Amr Musa, and by Arab commentators. The US step was viewed not only as "a Zionist defeat" but as further proof of American bias toward Israel and unconditional support "for its aggressive and racist practices."[55] The US positions on the issues of slavery and racism demonstrated its "double standards," claimed a Saudi newspaper,[56] as well as complete Zionist control over American decision making.[57]

Summing up the Arab performance in Durban, 'Amr Musa confided that he could not say that the Arabs had achieved all they had hoped for, "especially in regard to Israeli racist practices ... But we were able to shelve all references to the Holocaust, except one. We also made clear that there was hostility against Arabs and Islam."[58] Some Arab commentators took pride in the popular and NGO support for the Palestinian cause.[59] However, many felt that the conference had been hijacked and had ended with another Arab/Muslim defeat.[60] Nevertheless, the US had revealed its true face, wrote Walid Abu Zahr, and concluded, "Israel is a racist state whether this is stated in the Durban final declaration or not."[60]

Embracing Holocaust Deniers

In the wake of the intifada, crude Holocaust denial re-emerged as a means of delegitimizing Israel and Zionism, along with motifs that had typified the discourse of the early years of the Arab-Israeli conflict, such as regret that Hitler had not finished the job. Egyptian columnist Ahmad Rajab thanked Hitler for taking revenge on the Israelis "in advance on behalf of the Palestinians," but noted that it was not complete.[61] The PA semi-official paper *al-Hayat al-Jadida* published an article on 13 April by Khayri Mansur, entitled "Marketing Ashes," which elaborates various themes common to Holocaust deniers: alleged political and economic exploitation by Zionist propaganda, and doubting the number of Jews exterminated as well as well as the existence of the gas chambers.[62] The Hizballah website disseminated "The Holocaust Lie," from Richard Harwood's book *Did Six Million Really Die?*, and referred the browser to the Leuchter Report.[63] Norman Finkelstein's book *The Holocaust Industry* drew considerable attention in the Arab media. It was translated into Arabic, reviewed and discussed while Finkelstein himself was a welcome interviewee.[64] Although it does not deny the Holocaust, the book was perceived as an anti-Jewish/anti-Zionist tract, confirming Arab claims of exploitation of the Holocaust for Zionist political ends. At the Durban conference, Arab and Muslim representatives attempted, publicly, for the first time, to trivialize the Holocaust by denying its uniqueness and turning it into one of many holocausts.

The centrality of Holocaust denial in the Arab discourse was manifested in two events – an aborted conference of Western revisionists in Beirut, and an Arab forum on historical revisionism, which took place in May in Amman. The conference "Revisionism and Zionism," co-sponsored by the California-based Institute of Historical Review (IHR), the leading Holocaust denial group in the world, and by the Swiss-based Truth & Justice Association, was scheduled to be held between 31 March and 3 April in the Lebanese capital Beirut. Jürgen Graf, founder of Truth & Justice, who fled to Iran to avoid a 15-month prison sentence, was a driving force behind its organization. If it had taken place, it would have been the first such conference in the Middle East. The choice of the Middle East was not accidental. Undoubtedly, the organizers had wanted to exploit the anti-Israel mood in the Arab world to promote their cause. French Holocaust deniers Roger Garaudy and Robert Faurisson and German neo-Nazi Horst Mahler were among the scheduled speakers. No Arab participant was named in the program. Suspicions that Iran and Hizballah were behind the conference were never substantiated. In fact, the conference was not even mentioned in the Arab media until the US State Department intervened with the Lebanese government at the beginning of March, at the urging of three American Jewish organizations – the Wiesenthal Center, the World Jewish Congress and the ADL.[65]

Recognizing the potential damage to the Arab cause, a group of 14 Arab intellectuals – North Africans, Lebanese and Palestinians, including Colombia University professor Edward Said and poet Mahmud Darwish – published an open letter to Lebanese Prime Minister Rafiq Hariri calling for its cancellation. Arab Knesset member Ahmad Tibi also wrote to Hariri, urging the Arabs to reject any expression of understanding for Nazism, which had committed crimes against many peoples, including the Jews.[66] Most press criticism was expressed in Lebanese papers. In a harsh editorial entitled "The Protocols of the Elders of Beirut," prominent Lebanese writer Joseph Samaha branded the conference "a dishonor for Lebanon." Holding a conference of "falsifiers of history" in Lebanon, he warned, would be interpreted by Israel and its supporters "as prolonging the Nazi extermination project," which would harm the Palestinian cause and Palestinian victims.[67] Indeed the international pressure bore fruit and Hariri cancelled the conference on 23 March.[68] Lauding Hariri's decision the Lebanese *Daily Star* editorial argued that "few moves could place this country [Lebanon] in a poorer light than to host their [the revisionists'] detestable gathering. The very real challenges posed to the Arab world by the Jewish state demand far too much attention to let a cabal of hate-mongers distract the authorities in Lebanon or elsewhere in the region... Arguments about whether the Nazis murdered six million Jews or 'only' five million are legitimate but essentially irrelevant in the big picture... those who deny that the Holocaust took place at all are worthy of nothing but universal scorn."[69]

Hariri's statement canceling the Beirut conference neither mentioned the organizers' identity nor denounced their goals. Reaction in the Arab press and in the Lebanese parliament was divided: some supporting the conference and hence critical of the intellectuals' letter and the cancellation, and others opposing the conference. Generally, the public debate – as in previous cases such as the Garaudy affair in 1996 and 1998 (see *ASW 1996/7, 1998/9*) – revolved around the benefits that would have accrued to Zionism and Israel if the conference had taken place[70] as well as the potential damage to Lebanon and to the Palestinian cause.[71] "Denial of the Holocaust... is equivalent to denial of the Palestinian right of return... Moreover, it amounts to unjust exoneration of the Nazis, and might equally lead to denial of crimes committed by Israeli war criminals," wrote commentator 'Abd al-Wahhab Badrakhan.[72] On the other hand, the fourteen intellectuals were attacked for conceding unconditionally to the Zionist narrative and exerting pressure on Arab leaders to adopt their approach, while ignoring the adverse effects of their actions, such as infringement of freedom of speech.[73] Such attacks prompted Edward Said to retract; in a message dated 2 April, he explained that he had appended his signature to the letter "on condition that there would be no appeal to any government concerning a ban on the conference."[74] Similarly, three months later Mahmud Darwish claimed that the cancellation was "a violation of human rights and of the rights of scientific research of revisionist historians."[75]

In the context of this discussion, some commentators criticized the Arab attitude toward the extreme right in Europe. Lebanese writer Samir Kassir, for example, regretted that the Lebanese government had not seized the opportunity to explain to the world that the anti-Israel and anti-Zionist position had nothing to do with the racist atmosphere in Europe.[76] Yet, it seemed that increased usage in the Arab discourse of alleged Zionist exploitation of the Holocaust and the equation of Zionism with racism and Nazism converged with the revisionist discourse and argumentation. "The existence of the Zionist entity itself is not only a crime against the Arabs, but against humanity as well," concluded the statement of the Jordanian Writers Association on 10 April, denouncing the cancellation of the Beirut conference. Hence, "the liberation of humanity from neo-Nazism is its liberation from Zionism."[77]

The bitter controversy aroused by the intellectuals' letter as well as the cancellation of the conference culminated in an initiative to hold an alternative gathering in Amman. A group of Arab intellectuals, led by Ibrahim Alloush, a member of the Jordanian Writers Association (JWA) who had returned to Jordan after 13 years in the US, decided to organize a convention in Amman to discuss "what happened to the revisionist historians' conference in Beirut?" The meeting, which was postponed twice due to the intervention of Jordan's security authorities, finally took place, in cooperation with the Association against Zionism and Racism (AZAR), on 13 May to coincide with the commemoration of the Palestinian *nakba* (catastrophe – see *ASW 1998/9*). In contrast to the Beirut conference, where all the speakers were to have been Western Holocaust revisionists, the principal participants in the Amman meeting (150–200 participants in all) were Arab journalists and members of anti-normalization professional associations. They sought first and foremost to demonstrate opposition to the intellectuals who had called for the cancellation of the Beirut conference. The two main speakers were the Amman-based Lebanese journalist Hayat 'Atiyya and the Jordanian journalist 'Arafat Hijjazi. 'Atiyya (who appeared two days later on an al-Jazira talk show dealing with the question "Is Zionism Worse than Nazism?") emphasized the alleged parallels between Zionism and Nazism and argued that historical revisionism was not an ideology but a well-documented research project. Hijjazi dealt with common themes of Holocaust denial. The speakers also praised Roger Garaudy's contribution to popularizing "revisionism", outlined the speech Robert Faurisson had intended to deliver at the Beirut conference and proposed establishing an Arab Committee of Historical Revisionism.[78]

Although Arabs had embraced Holocaust denial in the past, the meeting in Amman may have been the first to signal a developing trend of cooperation between Arabs and revisionists. Ibrahim Alloush, who directs the *Free Arab Voice* site, asserted in an interview to the *Journal of Historical Review* that Arabs should be interested in the Holocaust and should take an active role in Holocaust revisionism. He argued that "most Arab regimes and leaders would not dare embrace "Holocaust" revisionism openly," but "the Arab world is fertile ground for revisionist seeds."[79]

SANCTIONING SUICIDE ATTACKS
The radicalization of the Arab attitude towards Israelis and Jews was reflected in religious edicts (*fatwas*) issued by Islamist leaders such as Usama bin Ladin, and by Palestinian muftis, ruling that killing Jews wherever they might be was a personal duty incumbent upon every Muslim. While these rulings – also issued in the past (see *ASW 1998/9, 2000/1*) – did not stir up any public debate, they apparently did succeed in mobilizing Palestinians, who carried out numerous terrorist attacks, including suicide bombings against Israeli and Jewish targets. The attacks occasionally triggered public debates, especially when they became counter-productive and harmed state interests. Such a discussion, which took place following the escalation in Palestinian suicide operations against innocent Israeli civilians during 2001 and before and after the September 11 attacks in the US, questioned their

Islamic legitimacy as well as their advisability. Although Palestinian suicide attacks were carried out only against Israeli targets as part of the Palestinian national struggle, Jews worldwide are potential targets, as in the bombing of the AMIA Jewish Center in Argentina in 1994 and more recently in Tunisia, where the ancient Jewish synagogue in Djerba was attacked in April 2002 by al-Qaʿida members. Investigations of a detainee in the US, accused of participating in the planning of the first attack on the World Trade Center in 1992, revealed that the perpetrators contemplated targeting Jewish sites in Brooklyn, but assumed that the operation was too complicated. Thus, the debate on suicide attacks, which in themselves do not always constitute acts deriving from antisemitism, is of an utmost relevance, since it reflects not only the Arab perception of the Arab-Israeli conflict but also of Jews in general.

The escalation of suicide operations within Israel was in itself an indication of the radicalized mood of the Palestinian street. Polls showed that support for these operations among the Palestinian population rose to about 80 percent in the course of the year.[80] The number of volunteers willing to sacrifice themselves "as a way to open the door to paradise for themselves and for their families" also mounted.[81] The recruits belonged not only to the Islamist movements – Hamas and Islamic Jihad – but also to the al-Aqsa brigades (members of the Tanzim, the secular PLO military wing) and even from among Israeli Arabs.[82] Moreover, they included women and teenagers.[83] Should suicide bombing be considered jihad? Were the perpetrators martyrs or simply terrorists, according to Islamic tradition? Should women and children take part in them? Did they serve Palestinian goals? What drove people to commit such acts? These were some of the questions raised in the debate, which encompassed Palestinian as well as other Arab religious scholars, intellectuals and politicians.

Traditional Islam forbids suicide and considers it to be a major sin. In addition, it forbids the killing of non-combatants, women, children and the elderly. However, from the mid-1990s Sunni Islamists adopted the Iranian/Shi'i concept of suicide missions and martyrdom. They used Qur'anic verses and Islamic oral tradition to sanction voluntary sacrifice of the self in the cause of Islam and Muslims, and to justify it as a martyrdom operation and a form of fulfilling the individual duty of jihad. Two approaches emerged in the debate: one argued that suicide bombings were "heroic acts of martyrdom" and "the supreme form of jihad for the sake of Allah," and the other delegitimized them as contradicting the spirit of Islam, especially since they targeted women and children.[84]

The debate in 2001 over the religious legitimacy of suicide attacks was triggered by an interview in *al-Sharq al-Awsat* with the mufti of Saudi Arabia Shaykh 'Abd al-'Aziz ibn 'Abdallah ibn Muhammad Al al-Shaykh, who ruled that suicide operations had no basis in Islamic law and did not constitute "jihad in the path of God." He also argued, four months before the September 11 events, that Islam forbade hijacking aircraft and terrorizing innocents.[85] Egypt's Shaykh al-Azhar Muhammad Sayyid Tantawi, also a government appointee, agreed with this ruling, excluding operations carried out against enemy soldiers.[86]

But these views immediately drew fire from most Palestinian religious scholars as well as from Shaykh Yusuf al-Qardawi, Hizballah religious leader Muhammad Husayn Fadlallah and radical al-Azhar scholars. They decreed that, to the contrary, martyrdom operations, a euphemism for suicide attacks, against occupation forces were permissible under Islamic law and constituted jihad. Al-Qardawi stressed that suicide operations against Israel were legitimate even if they killed civilians, and maintained that such martyrs could bring victory over the Zionist entity.[87] Egyptian pro-Islamist columnist Fahmi Huwaydi claimed he felt elation when a suicide bomber blew himself in a Jerusalem restaurant in August.[88] Expressing his loathing for the "racist Jewish entity," another Egyptian columnist advocated driving the Jews into the sea by acts of martyrdom, which would create "a balance of fear strategy." [89] There seemed to be a general consensus in Arab societies in favor of suicide operations, expressed in the high esteem bestowed upon those who carried them out and the financial rewards granted to their families.

The September 11 attacks in New York and Washington reopened the debate over suicide operations. Many Muslim clerics, including Husayn Fadlallah and Yusuf al-Qardawi, denounced the attacks, considering them terrorism and not martyrdom, since they were directed against innocent people who should not be held responsible for the deeds of the US administration.[90] The Islamic Research Council at al-Azhar issued a statement on 4 November, stating that "Islam provides clear rules and ethical norms that forbid the killing of noncombatants, as well as women, children, and the elderly."[91] A resolution in the same vein was adopted by the emergency meeting of foreign ministers of the Islamic Conference Organization, held in Doha, Qatar, in October.[92] But, a clear distinction was made between these attacks and suicide operations against Israeli targets, which were justified across the religious and political spectrum, since all Israelis were considered part of the Israeli war machine and "human bombs" were viewed as the most effective Muslim answer to the advanced Israeli arsenal of weapons.

However, a gradual shift in attitude was discerned, especially at the beginning of December, following another wave of suicide bombings in Israel. Several Arab commentators and Palestinians, such as cabinet member Ziyad Abu Ziyad and Fatah Higher Council secretary Marwan Barghuti, criticized them as counter-productive and harmful to the Palestinian cause.[93] Samir Kassir warned that "the Masada complex" threatens to emerge from Jewish history and storm the history of the Arabs, "as if enough damage has not been done already."[94] Egypt's Shaykh al-Azhar also backed down from his previous rulings, telling a group of foreign visitors that Islam condemned such attacks on innocent civilians,[95] only to be reprimanded by the mufti of Jerusalem, Shaykh Sabri 'Ikrima, who claimed that Tantawi's declarations were made under Egyptian and international pressure. Suicide attacks, he insisted, were legitimate means.[96]

As it turned out 'Ikrima's approach appeared to prevail, reflecting the overwhelming success of Islamist reasoning. Yet, it should be emphasized that Hamas and the Palestinian Islamic Jihad strongly opposed targeting Jews outside Israel. They claimed they were fighting the Zionist entity on the land of Palestine, or Israelis, not because they were Jews but because they were aggressors and occupiers.[97]

ANTISEMITIC MANIFESTATIONS IN THE WAKE OF 11 SEPTEMBER
The September 11 attacks on the World Trade Center in New York and the Pentagon in Washington by a group of radical Islamists instigated a wave of antisemitic manifestations, which exposed the strong linkage between anti-Americanism and antisemitism in the Arab and Muslim worlds. In the same way that the intifada reinforced Islamization of the conflict and the anti-Israeli discourse, bin Ladin and the Islamists brought about Islamization of the anti-American and anti-imperialist polemic. Hostility toward the Jews and Israel is part and parcel of the worldview of Usama bin Ladin and al-Qa'ida (the base) as well as of other Islamist movements, such as Hamas and Islamic Jihad. The struggle, or jihad, against "the Crusaders and the Jews" is a major theme in bin Ladin's ideology and constitutes the first stage in a long campaign for the restoration of the Muslim caliphate and the establishment of an Islamic world order. According to this view, the Jews are not only the occupiers of Muslim lands in Palestine but are part of Western Judeo-

Christian civilization, which is perceived as a threat to Islamic civilization and Islamic revival. Although seen also as the spearhead of the West in the war against Islam, the Jews and the issue of the Arab-Israeli conflict were not bin Ladin's first priority. Only when he felt during America's retaliatory war in Afghanistan that the Arab and Muslim demonstrations against the US were waning did he raise the Palestinian cause to the top of his agenda in his video addresses urging Muslims to action.[98]

The linkage between anti-Americanism and antisemitism was not confined to radical Islamists. It was abundantly demonstrated in Arab and Muslim reactions to the September 11 attacks. Several anti-Israel and antisemitic themes emerged in Arab press discussions of the events:

-Israeli intelligence was allegedly involved in the attacks.

-Jews had prior knowledge of the attacks.

-4,000 Jews were absent from work in the World Trade Center on that day.

-The American public had been misled by the dominant Israeli Zionists and by the strong influence of the Jewish lobby in the US.

-The Jews/Zionists vilified and demonized Muslims and instigated Islamophobia.

-Only Israel could benefit from such an act.

-Israel and the Jews wanted to drag the US and the West into a war against Islam.

-The Zionist enemy was practicing the ugliest forms of terrorism.

-If bin Ladin was guilty, he should be punished together with other terrorists, including Israeli Prime Minister Sharon.

All these themes reflected an instinctive response, which sought to transfer the blame from themselves to "the other," in this case, Israel. To Arab commentators the meticulously planned and executed operation seemed beyond the capabilities of an Arab/Muslim group. Conspiracy theories provided immediate explanations and answers to unresolved questions, and relieved Arab societies of self-examination and admission that they were the source of such destructive hatred and terrorism. Jews, Zionists or Israelis, the mythical conspirators, were portrayed by the Arab press – both mainstream and Islamic alike – as the masterminds behind the attacks. Upset by the blame attributed to Arabs and Muslims before any concrete evidence had been produced, some commentators argued that the international media, allegedly controlled by the Israeli/Jewish lobby, were responsible for the hatred toward them in the US and for covering up what they claimed was a Mossad operation.[99] Saudi prince Mamduh Bin 'Abd al-'Aziz, head of the Center for Saudi-Strategic Studies, claimed that whoever had read literature such as *The Protocols of the Elders of Zion* would know that the Jews were behind the international atmosphere of terror, and that they had infiltrated Islamist states and organizations.[100] Egyptian scholar Amira al-Shinwani also cited *The Protocols* as proof of the conniving Jewish character, as well as the fake document in which American President Benjamin Franklin allegedly warned of the dangers of Jewish immigration.[101] The Jews were not only capable of committing such an ugly crime, argued Jordanian columnist Rakan al-Majali, but no one would dare blame them because he would immediately be accused of perpetrating "a new Holocaust."[102] They conspired, plotted and used Arabs and Muslims as pawns, charged Muhammad Jami'a, an al-Azhar representative and imam in a New York Islamic center. In an interview from Cairo, to which he returned shortly after 11 September, he accused Jewish doctors in New York of poisoning sick Muslim children, and repeated all the allegations mentioned above. The interview was published on the Internet site of al-Azhar at the beginning of October.[103] "Israel drew maximum benefit from this terrorist activity," wrote Pakistani Islamist scholar Kurshid Ahmad. "A glance at the history of Israel and the Zionist movement gives credence to the suspicion of Mossad's role in the terrorist acts," he added. He also insinuated that Jews had known about the attacks since no Jewish names were found on the lists of the dead.[104]

The goal of the operations was to coerce the US and NATO "into submitting even further to Jewish Zionist ideology," by cultivating fears of "Islamic terrorism" and instigating a war against Islam.[105] "The Israelis and their Zionist propaganda worldwide had immediately seized on the pain and sorrow of the American people as an opportunity to incite the world against Islam and Muslims," wrote Palestinian Islamist scholar 'Azzam Tamimi in the pro-Hamas mouthpiece *Palestine Times* in October.

A few Arab writers and intellectuals, such as American Lebanese Professor Fu'ad 'Ajami, Pakistani Professor Akbar Ahmed in the US, Dean of Islamic Law at Qatar university, 'Abd al-Hamid al-Ansari, Kuwaiti university Professor Ahmad al-Baghdadi, Egyptian writer 'Ali Salim, and Lebanese writer Hazim Saghiya, however, not only condemned the attacks but also criticized Arab societies and regimes. They admitted that terrorist ideas fell on fertile ground in societies "ruled by a fanatic culture" which terrorizes its own citizens. They acknowledged that something has gone terribly wrong in a world where young men strap themselves with explosives, only to be hailed as martyrs. Arabs have nobody to blame but themselves for their misfortunes, and hence, should take a hard look in the mirror to mend their ways.[106]

CONCLUSION

"After the issue of terrorism, the question of 'Arabs and antisemitism' has returned to the headlines," wrote Lebanese liberal intellectual Hazim Saghiya, blaming Zionist zealots, Muslim clerics who justified the murder of Jews, and the Arab media.[107] Indeed, since the ongoing war between Israel and the Palestinians and the war against terrorism launched in the wake of the September 11 attacks had intensified the antisemitic discourse, Saghiya admitted that Arab antisemitism existed and "that it is powerful, even dangerous – and therefore must be fought." Books, speeches, television channels, statements and admiration for Holocaust deniers proved its existence; however, he argued, it was different from Christian antisemitism and lacked "the functional modernism of Nazism, the Nazi order, and the racist ideological adherence."

A contrary view was voiced by Jerome Slater, research professor at SUNY Buffalo, who claimed that "there is no basis for the assertion that Palestinian outrage at, or even hatred of, Israelis is a manifestation of traditional 'antisemitism'." It was rather a consequence of the Zionist dispossession of the Palestinians and "over fifty years of Israeli injustice and repression."[108] However, other scholars argue that this differentiation between antisemitism and anti-Zionism, or an anti-Israel position, seems increasingly invalid. In light of overwhelming anti-Israel manifestations worldwide, it may be perceived as "nothing but the old antisemitism in disguise."[109] "We in the West," contended senior editor Andrew Sullivan, "simply do not want to believe that this kind of hatred still exists; and when it emerges, we feel uncomfortable."[110]

Jewish and Israeli organizations and institutions are at the forefront of the struggle against Arab antisemitism. They reacted strongly to the planned Beirut conference, bringing about its cancellation (see above); attempted to abort the Amman meeting;[111] pressed the US administration to discuss antisemitism in the Egyptian press 'with President Husni Mubarak during his visit to the US in April;[112] and denounced Syrian President Asad's statements as well as the antisemitic satire on Abu Dhabi TV.[113] A new international forum for monitoring antisemitism launched in November and embracing Jewish and non-

Jewish organizations has placed Arab antisemitism at the top of its agenda.[114]

NOTES

All references are from 2001, unless otherwise stated.

1. Elia Awwad, "Perceiving the 'Other' in the al-Aqsa Intifada," *Palestine-Israel Journal* 2, p. 103.
2. *Ha'aretz*, 5 June.
3. Khalil Shikaki, "Old Guard, Young Guard: the Palestinian Authority and the Peace Process at a Cross Roads," 1 Nov. – msanews.mynet/shikaki.doc.
4. Khalil Shikaki, "Palestinian Attitudes during the Bush/Sharon Era," *PeaceWatch* 319, 20 April; *Jordan Times*, 2 May; *Ha'aretz*, 13 May.
5. *Ha'aretz*, 6 Feb.
6. *Ha'aretz*, 27 July.
7. *Ha'aretz*, 24, 27 April ; *Tishrin*, 24, 26 April ; *al-Hayat*, 25 April ; *Middle East Times*, 28 April ; *Azzaman*, 2 May ; *al-Ahram Weekly*, 3 May ; *al-'Arabi*, 6 May ; *Filastin al-Muslima*, June.
8. *al-'Arab al-Yawm*, 20 Jan..
9. *al-Ahram Weekly*, 3 May.
10. MEMRI, special dispatch no. 276, 25 Sept.
11. *al-Istiqlal*, 18, 25 Feb., 8 April; see also Itamar Marcus, Research Paper No. 37, 18 June, *Palestinian Media Watch*.
12. *Middle East Affairs* 1–2 (Winter/Spring), p. 215.
13. *Ma'ariv, sofshavoua'*, 23 Feb..
14. MEMRI, special dispatch no. 240, 11 July.
15. *al-Ahram*, 8 Feb. ; *The Economist*, 10 Feb. ; *Yedi'ot Aharonot*, 23 Feb. ; *Ha'aretz*, 7 March.
16. *al-Hayat*, 3 Feb.; *al-Usbu' al-Adabi*, 10 Feb.; *Tishrin*, 17 Feb.
17. *al-Akhbar*, 20 April.
18. *al-'Arab al-Yawm*, 14 Feb.; *Akhbar al-Yawm*, 17 Feb.; *al-Jumhuriyya*, 18 March; *al-Intifada*, 25 March).
19. *al-Usbu'*, 12 Feb.
20. *al-Intifada*, 11 Feb.
21. *al-Ahram*, 26 April; *Akhir Sa'a*, 27 April; *al-'Arabi*, 6 May; R. Damascus, 7 May; *Egyptian Mail*, 12 May; *Tishrin*, 13 Sept.
22. *al-Hayat*, 10 Feb.
23. *al-Ahram*, 8 Feb.; *al-Intifada*, 25 March.
24. *al-Ahram*, 12 Feb.

25. *al-Hayat*, 28 Jan.; *al-Ayyam*, 15 Feb.; *Filastin al-Muslima*, Feb.; *al-Ahram al-'Arabi*, 10 March; *Tishrin*, 9 April; *Syria Times*, 9 June.

26. *al-Nahar*, 23 March.

27. www.indictsharon.net.

28. *al-Hayat*, 19 Feb., 31 March; *al-Akhbar*, 20 April.

29. *al-Hayat*, 12 Jan.; *al-Istiqlal*, 18, 25 Jan., 29 March, 17 May; *Tishrin*, 20 Jan., 26 March; *October*, 28 Jan., 4 March; *al-Quds*, 29 Jan.; *al-Ahram*, 3, 14 Feb.; *al-Ayyam*, 15 Feb.; *Filastin al-Muslima*, March.

30. *Tishrin*, 24 Feb.

31. *Tishrin*, 20 Sept.

32. *al-Hayat al-Jadida*, 22 May; *Ha'aretz*, 23 May.

33. *al-Hayat*, 9 Jan.; *Ha'aretz*, 10 Jan.

34. *Tishrin*, *Ha'aretz*, 28 March; *al-Hayat*, 28, 29 March.

35. *Ha'aretz*, *al-Hayat*, 4 May.

36. *Tishrin*, 6, 7 May; *Ha'aretz*, 6, 7, 8 May; *Washington Post*, 7 May; *NYT*, 8, 13 May; *al-Hayat*, 8, 9, 12 May; *Jordan Times*, 9 May.

37. *Tishrin*, 15 May; *al-Hayat*, 21 May.

38. *Las Vegas Sun Online*, 5 May.

39. *al-Hayat al-Jadida*, 25 Jan.; see also *al-'Arab al-Yawm*, 12 Jan.; *al-Sabil*, 17 Aug.

40. *Washington Post*, 17 Dec.

41. *Ha'aretz*, 18, 21 Nov.; *Washington Post*, *New York Times*, 20 Nov.

42. *al-Hayat*, 12 Jan.; *al-Qahira*, 13 March; *Ha'aretz*, 30 March, 29 July .

43. *Ruz al-Yusuf*, 24 Feb.; *Middle East Times*, 10 March; MEMRI, special dispatch no. 190, 1 March; *Ha'aretz*, 29 March.

44. *al-Akhbar*, 25 March; MEMRI, special dispatch no. 201, 2 April.

45. *CSM*, 4 Sept.

46. *Ha'aretz*, 24 Sept.

47. *al-Ahram al-'Arabi*, 24 Feb.; *Annashra*, April; *al-Istiqlal*, 2 Aug.

48. *al-Istiqlal*, 24 March.

49. *al-Usbu' al-Adabi*, 5 May.

50. *al-Sharq al-Awsat*, 18, 21, 22, 23 July; *al-Ahram al-'Arabi*, 21 July; *al-Hayat*, 23 July.

51. *al-Sharq al-Awsat*, 1, 4, 27 Aug..

52. *Middle East Affairs Journal* 1-2 (Winter/Spring), pp. 235–9.

53. Michael Colson, "Durban and the Middle East: Challenges for US Policy," *PolicyWatch* 548, 1 Aug.; *al-Sharq al-Awsat*, 10, 16 Aug.; *al-Ba'th*, 26 Aug.; *Tishrin*, 1, 3, 4, 6, 8 Sept.; *al-Akhbar*, 2 Sept..

54. *Tishrin*, 3 Sept.; South Africa News Agency (SAPA), 8 Sept.

55. MENA, 4 Sept.; *Tishrin*, 5, 6, 9 Sept.; *Syria Times*, 8 Sept..

56. *Jedda Arab News Online*, 2, 19 Aug.

57. *Tehran Times*, 5 Sept.

58. *al-Sharq al-Awsat*, 3 Sept.; *Ha'aretz*, 4 Sept.; *al-Zaman*, *al-Hayat*, 7 Sept.; *al-Siyasa al-Duwaliya*, Oct.

59. *Keyhan International*, 1 Sept.; *al-Akhbar*, 3 Sept.; *al-Sharq al-Awsat*, 7, 9 Sept.; *al-Ahram al-'Arabi*, *al-Mujtama'*, 15 Sept.

60. *al-Watan al-'Arabi*, 14 Sept.; see also *al-Sunna*, *Filastin al-Muslima*, Oct.

61. *al-Akhbar*, 25 April; AJC Press Release, 3 June; ADL, "Holocaust Denial in the Middle East: The Latest Anti-Israel Propaganda Theme," nd - adl.org.

62. *Jerusalem Post*, 18, 19 April; 8 June; *Ma'ariv*, 19 April.

63. resistance.homepage.com.

64. *al-Ahram al-'Arabi*, 24 February; *al-Sharq al-Awsat*, 13 March; *al-Hawadith*, 16 March; *al-Adab*, March-April; *Annashra*, April; *Daily Star*, 3 July.

65. US Newswire, *JP*, 12 Feb.; *Ma'ariv*, *Ha'aretz*, 13 Feb.; ihr.org/conference/beirutconf; *Tishrin*, 24 Feb.; *al-Nahar*, *al-Safir*, 3 March; *Tehran Times*, 4 March.

66. *Le Monde*, 15 March; *Ha'aretz*, 19, 20, 23 March.

67. *al-Hayat*, 13 March; *Le Monde*, 15 March.

68. *al-Nahar*, 23, 24 March; *JP*, 23, 25 March; *al-Hayat*, 24, 25 March; *Daily Star*, 24, 26 March; *Ha'aretz*, 25, 29 March.

69. *Daily Star*, 24 March.

70. *al-Nahar*, 20 March; *al-Wasat*, 26 March.

71. *al-Nahar*, 20, 23 March.

72 *al-Hayat*, 19 March.

73. *al-Anwar*, 21 March; *al-Akhbar*, 13 April; Ibrahim Alloush, "Between Public Relations and Self-Alienation: Arab Intellectuals and the 'Holocaust'," *Journal of Historical Review* (May/June).

74. ihr.org/conference/beirutconf.

75. *MSANEWS*, 16 July.

76. *al-Nahar*, 23 March.

77. ihr.org/conference/beirutconf.

78. *Free Arab Voice Online* (FAV), 15, 28 April; *JP*, 17, 23 April, 22 May; *al-Safir*, 20 April; *Jordan Times Online*, 15 May; *al-Hayat al-Jadida*, 15 May; al-Jazira TV, 15 May – MEMRI, dispatch no. 225, 6 June; *Middle East News Online*, 16 May; AZAR, 18 May – *MSANEWS*.

79. "Why the 'Holocaust' Is Important to Palestinians, Arabs and Muslims? *FAV*, 28 April; *The Journal of Historical Review* (May/June); see also Alloush' series of articles published in Islamist weekly *al-Sabil*, 1–22 May.

80. *Ha'aretz*, 13 May; AFP, 3 June; *Jerusalem Report*, 22 Oct..

81. MEMRI, Inquiry and Analysis, no. 61, 25 June; *New York Post*, 9 Dec..

82. MEMRI, special dispatch no. 260, 22 Aug.; *Jerusalem Report*, 19 Nov.

83. *Jerusalem Post*, 15 Aug.; *Independent*, 22 Aug..

84. Yotam Feldner, "The Debate over Religious Legitimacy," MEMRI, Inquiry and Analysis, no. 53, part 1, 2 May; part, 2, 3 May; no. 65; part 3, 26 July; *Los Angeles Times*, 22 Aug.; David Zeidan, "The Islamic Fundamentalist View of Life as a Perennial Battle," *Middle East Review of International Affairs (MERIA) Journal*. 4 (Dec.).

85. *al-Sharq al-Awsat*, 21 April; *Ha'aretz*, 11 May; 3 June.

86. *al-Hayat*, 27 April.

87. *al-Ahram*, 24, 26 April; *al-'Arab al-Yawm*, 25 April; *al-Hayat*, 25, 27 April, 11 May; *Islamic Association for Palestine (IAP) News*, 26 April; *al-Liwa'*, 2 May; *al-Istiqlal*, 26 April, 14, 28 June; *al-Sabil*, 1 May; *Ruz al-Yusuf*, 4 May; *Filastin al-Muslima*, May.

88. *al-Ahram*, 14 Aug.; MEMRI, special dispatch, no.265, 31 Aug.

89. *al-Usbu'*, 28 May; MEMRI, special dispatch no. 224, 4 June.

90. *al-Ahram al-'Arabi*, 20 Oct.; *al-Ahram Weekly*, 6 Dec.; interview with Shaykh Muhammad Husayn Fadlallah, *Journal of Palestine Studies*. 2 (Winter 2002), p. 80.

91. *New York Review*, 17 Jan. 2002.

92. *Yedi'ot Aharonot*, 11 Oct.

93. *Ha'aretz*, 24 Aug.; *al-Watan*, 12 Sept.; *NYT*, 5 Dec.; *al-Quds*, 7 Dec.; *al-Watan*, 10 Dec. [*Mideast Mirror*]; *al-Hayat*, 12 Dec. [*Mideast Mirror*].

94. *al-Nahar*, 10 Dec. [*Mideast Mirror*].

95. *al-Ahram*, 4 Dec.; *al-Ahram Weekly*, 6 Dec.; *Ha'aretz*, 6, 7, 19 Dec.

96. *al-Hayat*, 7 Dec.; *Ha'aretz*, 9 Dec.

97. Ahmad Yasin, in Internet chat, *Islam Online*, 1 April; *al-Istiqlal*, 5 April; *al-Mujtama'*, 22 Sept.

98. *Yedi'ot Aharonot*, 16 Sept.; *NYT*, 9 Dec.; *al-Sharq al-Awsat*, 2–12 Dec.

99. *al-Dustur*, *al-Ra'y*, *al-Akhbar*, 13 Sept.; al-Manar TV, 15 Sept. [BBC]; *al-Ayyam*, *al-'Arabi*, 16 Sept.; *al-Istiqlal*, 4 Oct.; *al-Ahram*, 7 Oct.; CSM, 6 Nov.

100. *al-Hayat*, 24 Sept.

101. *al-Ahram*, 26 Oct.

102. *al-Dustur*, 13 Sept.

103. lailatalqadr.com.

104. Kurshid Amad, "Elimination of Terrorism or Beginning of New Crusades," *Tarjuman al-Qur'an*, Oct. [MSANEWS]; see also: *Star*, 20 Sept.; *al-Sabil*, 24 Sept.

105. *al-Sabil*, 2 Oct.

106. *al-Hayat*, 15 Sept.; *al-Sharq al-Awsat*, 17 Sept., 21 Dec.; MEMRI, no. 298, 8 Nov.; no. 302, 20 Nov.; no. 307, 4 Dec.; nos. 337, 338, 29, 30 Jan. 2002).

107. *al-Hayat*, 12 Dec.; MEMRI, special dispatch no. 314, 14 Dec.

108. Jerome Slater, "Israel, Antisemitism and the Palestinian Problem," *Tikkun* (May–June) [MSANEWS].
109. Hillel Halkin, "The Return of Anti-Semitism," *Commentary*, Feb. 2002.
110. *The New Republic*, 5 Nov.
111. *JP*, 3 May; *al-Sabil*, 8 May.
112. *Ha'aretz*, 2 April.
113. *al-Hayat*, 15 June; *Ma'ariv*, 18 June; *Jerusalem Post*, 19 Nov.
114. *Ma'ariv*, 19 Nov.

The Jedwabne Affair

Robert S. Wistrich§

A specter has been haunting Poland since the turn of the millennium – that of Jedwabne, a town of just over 2,000 inhabitants in the province of Mazowsze, about 100 kilometers northeast of Bialystok. On a hot summer day, 10 July 1941, a massacre of Jews was perpetrated in this remote region of northeast Poland. Within a few hours virtually all of Jedwabne's 1,600 Jews – men, women and small children – were wiped out, in broad daylight, by their Polish neighbors. This last fact – that the actual perpetrators were not German Nazis but "ordinary Poles" – stunned many in Poland with the publication there of Jan Gross's book *Neighbors* in May 2000. For as this slim volume makes clear, the invading Germans played at best a secondary role in Jedwabne – though without their presence, encouragement or approval it is difficult to imagine such events having taken place. Nevertheless, it was the local inhabitants (all members of the Polish ethnic community) who voluntarily carried out the killings, under the direction of Mayor Marian Karolak, and with the active participation of the entire town council.

Jan Gross identified no fewer than 92 Jedwabne residents who actively took part in the murders (some of whom he interviewed), and he claims that everyone in the town "either participated in or witnessed the tormented deaths of the Jews of Jedwabne." Hence, he regards these events as a mass murder in a dual sense, "on account of both the number of victims and the number of perpetrators." By revealing that the killers were Poles he challenged not only the earlier Polish investigations into what had happened at Jedwabne (the commemorative inscription erected by the Communist regime blames the Gestapo and "Nazi and gendarmerie") but also Poland's self-image concerning the wartime years and the Holocaust.[1]

Although it took sixty years to uncover the stark truth about Jedwabne, many details had already come to light much earlier. For example, here is part of the testimony of an eye-witness (Szmul Wasersztajn) recorded in April 1945 and deposited in the Jewish Historical Institute in Warsaw:

---

§ Robert Wistrich is professor of European history at the Hebrew University of Jerusalem and chairman of the Vidal Sassoon International Center for the Study of Antisemitism.

... local hooligans armed themselves with axes, special clubs studded with nails, and other instruments of torture and destruction and chased all the Jews into the street. As the first victims of their devilish instincts they selected seventy-five of the youngest and healthiest Jews, whom they ordered to pick up a huge monument of Lenin that the Russians had erected in the center of town. It was impossibly heavy, but under a rain of horrible blows the Jews had to do it. While carrying the monument, they also had to sing until they brought it to the designated place. They were ordered to dig a hole and throw the monument in. Then the Jews were butchered to death and thrown into the same hole.[2]

This was only a part of the almost indescribable ordeal that the Jews of Jedwabne were forced to endure on that burning hot summer's day just six decades ago.

Beards of old Jews were burned, newborn babies were killed at their mothers' breasts, people were beaten murderously and forced to sing and dance. In the end they proceeded to the main action – the burning. The entire town was surrounded by guards so that nobody could escape; then Jews were ordered to line up in a column, four in a row, and the ninety year old rabbi and the *shochet* were put in front. They were given a red banner and all were ordered to sing and chased into the barn.... Then the barn was doused with kerosene and lit, and the bandits went around to search Jewish homes, to look for the remaining sick and children.[3]

These and other surviving accounts tell a story of mayhem, mutilation and murder. Some Jews were knifed and left to bleed to death, others had their bodies pierced with sharp instruments; babies were thrown to the ground and trampled to death; men had their eyes or tongues cut out – many had their throats slashed. Groups of Jews were forced to undress and perform ridiculous exercises to the jeers and applause of the watching crowd, which included women and children. The Jews gathered in the market square of Jedwabne and already reeling from savage blows and the effects of scorching thirst, were made to chant: "The war is because of us, the war is for us."

This was the grim prelude to their being burned alive in local farmer Edward Slezynski's barn – their screams of agony drowned out by the sounds of music. Neither the smell of burning flesh nor the dark smoke billowing over the small town appears to have dampened the enthusiasm of the onlookers who witnessed this gruesome spectacle.

At the original trial held in Lomza in May 1949 (there was a sequel in 1953), the Polish Communist authorities did indict twenty residents of Jedwabne for "aiding and abetting the German occupiers." Ten were acquitted altogether but other defendants received sentences ranging from eight to fifteen years, though most were released without serving their full time. There was only one death sentence, which was subsequently commuted.[4]

Gross used the trial records extensively, relying on the perpetrators' own accounts as well as the testimony of the few Jewish survivors. Subsequently, on visiting Jedwabne, he learned that the whole story was well documented, that witnesses were still alive, and that the memory of the crime had been preserved in Jedwabne through the generations. The evidence was there but there was unwillingness to integrate it into Polish national memory.[5] A breakthrough occurred when some Jedwabne residents agreed to be interviewed by filmmaker Agnieszka Arnold in 1998 for her documentary *Dzie jest moj brat Kain?* (Where is my brother, Cain?) which was aired on the main channel of Polish State Television in April 2000. The interviews essentially confirmed Gross's findings, as did two serious articles (to which he pays tribute in his book) by investigative reporter Andrzej Kaczynski, which appeared in *Rzeczpospolita* (5 and 19 May 2000). Kaczynski's first piece, entitled "Calopalenie" (Holocaust or "Burning Alive"), was devoted exclusively to the Jedwabne massacre, which the journalist cautiously described as instigated by Germans but executed "by Polish hands." The reporter confessed that he had encountered much xenophobia and antisemitism in the course of his enquiries; but one essential point was made abundantly clear. "Not only old people, but even young people who knew the truth from family sources... told me that Jews were put to a cruel death first of all by the Poles. I was also told that some of the murderers are still alive."

Jedwabne was not the only small town in Poland where Jews were taunted, beaten, stabbed and then burned alive in a barn. Something similar had happened in neighboring Radzilow on 7 July 1941 where 800 Jews were killed, three days before the horrifying events in Jedwabne. Gross devotes a chapter to this precedent. Other massacres apparently took place in the same period in Wasosz and Stawiski in the same region as Jedwabne. The Germans themselves had provided the model by burning Jews alive in a synagogue in Bialystok on 27 June 1941 (an incident which Gross does not mention) just five days after the attack on the Soviet Union. This raises questions that some of Gross's critics pointedly asked. Did he not underplay the role of the Germans in organizing so-called self-cleansing actions by embittered and antisemitic Poles? How many Germans were in fact present in Radzilow and Jedwabne on the crucial days? What did they do or say? Did they order Poles to kill Jews, give them a green light to do so, or simply stand by and let them get on with what they ardently wished to do anyway? German archives apparently do indicate the presence in the region of an *Einsatzgruppe* led by Hermann Schaper who (according to government historian Pawel Machcewicz) was in Radzilow on 7 July – the day of the massacre. That may be significant. However, even if some direct German involvement were proven, it would not exonerate the Poles. As one resident of Radzilow, Mariusz Gryczkowski, put it: "I feel sorry and sad about all this. It makes me not want to be a Pole... When the Russians were here the Jews had contacts with them and denounced some people, and people were deported. When the Germans were here Jews were in a bad situation. And when the Russians were here Poles were in a bad situation. That's the bottom line of the story. But it shouldn't have happened."[6]

However, the mayor of neighboring Radzilow, Kazimierz Gwiazdowski, a 38-year-old farmer, seems unrepentant, skeptical and even dismissive of Gross's account: "I don't think a book should be written based on one story. I can invent any story right now."[7] For the present, Radzilow's memorial still stands, with its misleading Communist-era plaque that states: "In August 1941 fascists murdered 800 people of Jewish nationality, and among those, 500 were burned alive in a barn." Many of its residents seem reluctant to face the more painful truth of Polish involvement.

The Polish Catholic Church has also found it difficult to speak with one voice in the face of the recent revelations. Not for the first time, different and even opposing trends within its ranks have emerged. For example, Bishop Stanislaw Stefanek of Łomża declared that the people of this destitute region of northeast Poland were essentially innocent and described the media interest as an American conspiracy to defame Poles. Such comments were echoed by the notoriously antisemitic Reverend Henryk Jankowski (former confessor to Lech Walesa), who even created a model of the Jedwabne barn in his own church to symbolize attempts to blame Poles for the atrocity. On the other hand, the Catholic monthly *Więz* (Bond) published an impressive collection of articles on the current debate entitled "Thou Shalt Not Kill. Poles on Jedwabne." In his introduction to the volume, now translated into English, the former chief historian of Yad Vashem, Israel Gutman, writes:

These people knew each other's names and faces, they knew their neighbors' parents and children, had worked together in order to survive the difficult times.... This massacre – committed only because the victims were Jews – is an unheard of, incomprehensible atrocity."[8]

The Polish perpetrators, he observes, were neither uniformed ruffians nor "collaborators" of the Germans. There were no local conflicts or specific events with inflammatory consequences that might provide an "explanation" for the orgy of destruction that took place. Gutman suggests that while the lawless savagery and disregard for human life imposed by Nazi rule was the trigger for the tragedy, it could not have happened without the widespread hostility to Jews in pre-war Poland, which stigmatized them as an existential threat that had to be eliminated.[9]

There has been considerable soul-searching among more enlightened Poles since the publication of Gross's book. It has not been easy for a nation accustomed to think of itself as a victim of history to suddenly see itself as directly implicated in the mass murder of Jews. Poles pride themselves on having had the largest resistance movement in occupied Europe. They point out that their country had been brutally occupied, both by Hitler's Wehrmacht and by the Red Army in September 1939. They believe that they fought Nazism with all their might until the last day of the war and certainly they suffered terrible casualties in the process. Nearly three million ethnic Poles (ten percent of the overall Polish population) and about three million Polish Jews were killed during the war (ninety per cent of the pre-war Jewish population). If we include the Jews, then Poland lost six million people or twenty percent of its former inhabitants in six years of uninterrupted horror.

Poles also take pride in the fact that they did not produce Quislings or collaborators on anything like the scale that existed across Europe between 1939 and 1945. Until the revelations concerning Jedwabne, Radzilow, and a few other small towns in the Bialystok region, it was widely believed that Polish hands were relatively clean of mass killing of Jews. The fact remains that Poles did not engage, on the whole, in the savage murders of Jews, as did the Lithuanians, Latvians, Ukrainians, Romanians, Hungarians, Croats and other collaborators of the Germans during the war years.[10] They did not send regiments to the Eastern Front to fight with the Wehrmacht or the Waffen-SS; and there were relatively few Poles who served as guards in the concentration or death camps.

Moreover, there are more Polish names in the Avenue of Righteous Gentiles at Yad Vashem than those of any other nationality.

But all too often in the past these valid arguments (and other less legitimate ones) have been used selectively and tendentiously to deny any kind of Polish responsibility for the Shoah. This was already apparent in an earlier Polish controversy about the Holocaust sparked by the literary critic Professor Jan Blonski, who was highly critical of his countrymen's distorted and apologetic stance towards the annihilation of the Jewish people.[11] The debate, carried on initially in the important Catholic publication *Tygodnik Powszechny*, focused on a different (though related) set of issues, such as the Polish failure to do more to rescue Jews and the blight of antisemitism in Polish political life before the war, during the Holocaust itself, and in its aftermath. Even highly sensitive subjects such as the heinous deeds of the *szmalcownicy* (Poles who turned Jews over to the Germans in return for money), the transfer during wartime of Jewish property to Polish as well as German hands and the collaboration of the Polish "blue police" (*granatowej policji*) with the Nazis, were discussed in this internal debate of the late 1980s.

There were those who pointed out that the flattering self-image of Poles as ardent patriots, underground fighters and knights in shining armor was somewhat misleading when it came to Jews. True, reproaches often heard in the outside world that all Poles were endemically antisemitic might be unjust, but (as the critics noted) Polish silence, denial and opportunism during and after the Shoah had contributed to this image. Polish historiography had timidly avoided subjects such as the three thousand or so Jews murdered by Polish antisemitic gangs and by members of the underground Polish Home Army during the Holocaust and after the war. Under the Communists, a veil of silence still hung thickly over most Polish historical writing on these subjects, leaving only self-serving nationalist assertions about Polish heroism and the "generous help" allegedly given the Jews.[12] Self-criticism, where it existed, generally came from dissidents, particularly among Catholic intellectuals in Krakow.

Jan Gross – professor of politics and European studies at New York University –came from a very different background to Blonski. Born into a thoroughly assimilated mixed family (his father was a prominent lawyer and his paternal grandfather served as a liberal Jewish deputy for Krakow in the Imperial Austrian parliament), he left the country as a young man after the Polish student unrest of 1968 and brief imprisonment, to settle in the United States. Though his half-Jewish origins have not passed unnoticed by his more antisemitic critics, there is no reference to this personal background in his book. He was very clearly writing as a Pole addressing his compatriots over a matter of common national concern. His aim was not simply to reveal the identity of the perpetrators of the Jedwabne atrocity but to shake the conscience of his readers so that "the new generation, raised in Poland with freedom of speech and political liberties, is ready to confront the unvarnished history of Polish-Jewish relations during the war."[13]

From a methodological viewpoint, Gross sharply rejected the idea of "two separate wartime histories – one pertaining to the Jews and the other to all of the other citizens of a given European country subjected to Nazi rule." In his view, it was self-evident that "when the Polish half of a town's population murders its Jewish half, we have on our hands an event patently invalidating the view that these two ethnic groups' histories are disengaged."[14]

Gross resolutely opposes the classic Polish apologetic argument which "explains" the Jedwabne massacre as revenge for alleged Soviet-Jewish "collaboration" before the German invasion. According to this theory – still very popular in Poland – when the Red Army entered the eastern half of the country in mid-September 1939, it had been enthusiastically welcomed by the Jewish population. Not only Catholic nationalists, ultra-rightists and open antisemites espouse this myth but also prominent historians such as Professor Tomasz Strzembosc of the Catholic University of Lublin. According to Strzembosc, an expert on the eastern region of Poland, Jews took part en masse in enforcing the new Soviet order. Not only did they replace ethnic Poles in local offices but, so he claimed in *Rzeczpospolita*, they helped deport Poles to Siberia and northern Kazakhstan. "This was collaboration with arms in hand, taking the side of the enemy, treason in days of defeat."[15]

By evoking this allegedly "treacherous" collaboration, Professor Strzembosc and others appear to be trying to create an artificial symmetry and even a spurious moral equivalent to the Holocaust. Even if it were proven that Jews collaborated with the NKVD (Soviet secret police) in significantly higher numbers than Poles, Ukrainians or Belorussians – could this possibly justify Polish citizens clubbing, drowning, gutting and burning their Jewish neighbors to death in Jedwabne? Moreover, did Jews under the Soviet occupation actually kill or murder any Polish soldiers or civilians? I know of no single documented case of any Jew executing or burning Poles alive under Soviet rule. Gross himself, who is an expert also on the "sovietization" of Western Ukraine and Western Belorussia, points out in *Neighbors* (and in earlier works) that more Poles than Jews actually collaborated with the

Russians – including in the Jedwabne region.[16] Furthermore, one-third of all Polish citizens deported eastwards to the interior of the Soviet Union, many ending up in Stalinist labor camps, were in fact Jews, and they included my parents who were deported from Lviv in eastern Poland in June 1940, after fleeing there from Krakow.

My own family history is as good a refutation of the Polish myth of "Soviet-Jewish collaboration" and *Zydo-Komuna* (Judeo-communism) as any pseudo-scientific argument disseminated by Gross's critics.[17] Both of my parents sympathized before 1939 with the Polish democratic left as a result of the increasingly rampant antisemitism in Polish society. Like many Jews, they had little reason to admire the Polish Republic, after having lived for two decades under its discriminatory practices. In the Soviet Union, they naïvely believed, Jews were not second-class citizens but enjoyed genuine equality. However, shortly after encountering the Soviet system in Lviv in 1940 my parents were rapidly disillusioned by its mendacity, corruption and ruthlessness. My father discovered that his "bourgeois" class origins made him suspect in the eyes of the Soviet authorities, as did the social background of many Jewish merchants, traders and professional people in eastern Poland.

My mother was more fortunate since the Soviets put her in charge of a horticulture institute in Lviv, which made a pleasant change after being denied employment as a "Jewess" in pre-war Poland. But like other inhabitants of the region, she learned that Soviet rule meant rapid "proletarianization" of all living standards and exposure to completely arbitrary decrees. Subsequently, my parents were deported eastwards, experiencing conditions identical to those of Poles in the Soviet Gulag. They arrived in Kazakhstan in 1942, where my father was twice imprisoned by the NKVD – the second time on fabricated charges of "anti-Soviet" propaganda. I mention this in order to illustrate the misleading character of the Polish myth of Judeo-communism whose extraordinary tenacity was once more revealed in the Jedwabne affair. Out of the 3.2 million Jews living in pre-war Poland, no more than several thousand were members of the outlawed Communist Party. Moreover, after 1945 even those who loyally served in the Party and its security apparatus did so as Communists not as Jews. They did not serve any "Jewish" interest. Yet the antisemitic stereotype has survived the war and continues to flourish, revived by historians such as Strzemboscz, Marek Jan Chodakiewicz and the head of the National Remembrance Institute Board Dr. Slavomir Radon, who openly wondered to what degree the motive for the murders at Jedwabne was revenge for the Jewish population's "collaboration" with the Soviet authorities."[18]

Another familiar bogey resurfaced in the Jedwabne debate – that of "anti-Polonism," this time in the guise of an organized conspiracy to lay responsibility for the Holocaust at Poland's door. Jerzy Robert Nowak writing in *Nasz Dziennik* (May 2000) crudely dismissed Gross's book as "the usual propaganda to get out of the Polish government money for the crimes committed in Poland by Germans, Soviets and criminals [*Kryminalistow*]."[19] This was echoed by Leszek Czajkowki in *Nasza Polski* and by others writing in the right-wing, Catholic-nationalist and antisemitic press, which reaches hundreds of thousands of readers.[20]

The American Jewish radical Norman G. Finkelstein, in an unbridled and slanderous attack on Gross's book, which appeared in abridged form in *Rzeczpospolita* (20 June 2001), added his own inflammatory gloss to the Polish debate. He claimed that Gross was merely a pale caricature of Daniel Goldhagen, and that his writing bore "the unmistakable imprint of the Holocaust industry" – supposedly out to exploit the Jewish genocide for political and financial gain. What particularly aroused Finkelstein's onslaught was the chapter on stolen Jewish property which Gross linked to Polish antisemitism and the Holocaust. Gross's suggestion that Poles must deal with the moral and material consequences of the past was (according to Finkelstein) especially offensive and cynical, since he had no right to lecture Poland from the comfort of New York City. "What sacrifices will he [Gross] suffer if the Holocaust industry bankrupts Poland?" – Finkelstein rhetorically asked his Polish readers. According to Finkelstein himself, no American professor who was silent about US crimes and no Israeli who failed to denounce Zionist "crimes against peace" had the right to confront the Poles with their past.

Were it not for this pitiful level of argument, the spectacle of Norman Finkelstein echoing the most reactionary Polish antisemites in his diatribes against the "Holocaust industry," might almost be amusing. But for xenophobic chauvinist Poles, such a critique confirmed their fury at the "malicious" propaganda campaign (centered in Manhattan) to have Poles, rather than Germans, identified as Holocaust perpetrators. For the radical right, the "lying Jewish enemy" of Poland (supported by treacherous Polish lackeys) can never change his spots – driven as he is by relentless greed, hatred of Poles and willingness to employ blackmail to squeeze reparations from its "innocent" prey.[21]

More typical, however, of the scholarly critics has been the charge that *Neighbors* is a sensationalist work. Allegedly, it does not meet accepted scholarly standards and contains "one-sided testimonies" and "premature" conclusions. Marek Chodakiewicz, for instance, accused

Gross of treating facts nonchalantly, of dilettantism, irresponsibility, and employing an unduly emotional style (the tone of the book is in fact remarkably sober).[22] Such charges could, however, have been better applied to Chodakiewicz himself since he provided little evidence for his assumption that those murdered in Jedwabne were accomplices of the NKVD. Others cast doubt on the reliability of any Jewish eye-witnesses to the atrocity, claiming that they lacked the necessary detachment to be "calm and objective observers."[23] The Polish historian Thomas Szarota also spoke for many "skeptics" when he suggested that the Poles must have been egged on by German troops or the SS. No conclusions, he insisted, could be drawn until a full investigation of all German archives had been completed.[24] Thus far, at any rate, these archives have not contradicted anything which Gross wrote.

Despite the various "scientific" reproaches voiced, it is important to note that none of the historians (or more serious critics) actually denied the facts per se. There was a general consensus that Gross's book did puncture the Polish self-image.[25] One could no longer claim that Poles had kept their hands clean in a just war, totally innocent of Hitler's crimes. For Gross's supporters, this demystification has been liberating. Writing in *Gazeta Wyborcza* (2–3 Dec. 2000), the anthropologist Joanna Tokarska-Bakir reproached Polish historians for being "over-cautious" and "non-controversial" in their desire to be taken seriously [*poważny*]." Why, for example, did they only begin to address taboo subjects such as Jedwabne after Gross had completed his investigation? Why had Polish historians waited until the last eye-witnesses were on the verge of disappearing before seriously dealing with the Holocaust? Was it not time to investigate why at the end of the war in 1946 Poles were still killing Jews in their own country and pushing survivors to leave Poland forever? How was such antisemitism possible at all after everything that had happened during the Shoah?[26] These and many other questions are now being asked.

The editor of *Gazeta Wyborcza*, Adam Michnik, frankly acknowledged that he felt a certain "schizophrenia" and even guilt as a Pole "responsible to the world for the evil inflicted by my countrymen" and as a Jew who would certainly have been killed had he been there. In a revealing article, he wrote of the "deep trauma which surfaces with each new debate about antisemitism, Polish-Jewish relations and the Holocaust"; the feeling of guilt among Poles at having been helpless witnesses to atrocity, at profiting in many cases from the Jewish tragedy and at the many falsifications of history to which the Holocaust had been subjected in postwar Poland. The murders in Jedwabne, he concluded, had been further aggravated by denial of the truth about them for so many decades and he reproached himself for not seeking it out more energetically; perhaps, Michnik speculated, he had "subconsciously feared the cruel truth about the Jewish fate during that time."[27]

Even bolder in his approach was the current president of Poland, Alexander Kwasniewski, himself a former communist, who in the spring of 2001 spoke publicly of "the black stains" in Polish history, which "we will no longer be able to ignore... with all the pain, they must be exposed and not plastered over." He insisted that "whatever the background may be to this horrible deed, one thing must not be forgotten: it was a mass murder of Jews by Poles... There must be heard from our mouths, the mouths of the Poles, a request for forgiveness and pardon from the Jews."[28]

Poland's National Remembrance Institute opened its own investigation, exhuming the mass graves and interviewing witnesses. The institute's chairman, Leon Kieres, frankly declared on Polish radio: "As a Pole, I can't shake off the blame for what has happened." Repeatedly, in interviews with the press, he emphasized that "the most important thing is the truth."[29]

Even a few residents of Jedwabne, such as Stanislaw Michalowski, read *Neighbors* and seem to have been strongly affected. He told reporters that he was no longer the same man. "We were raised in the conviction that we Poles were clean during the war, that atrocities had nothing to do with us. It's morally crushing to realize what happened."[30] But there have been other voices too, and most of Jedwabne's present population feel little connection with the past or a sense of responsibility for the July 1941 massacre. The current mayor, Krzysztof Kodlewski, a 45-year-old schoolteacher, received many threatening phone calls as a result of his own praiseworthy efforts at honesty, frankness and reconciliation. He openly voiced the fear that his own children could become antisemites "when they are accused of being the children of murderers."[31]

Some elderly Jedwabne residents still repeat the old canard that during the war Poles were sent to Siberia "because of the Jews." The local Catholic priest, Edward Orlowski, even claimed that "what happened in Jedwabne was a battle against communists and not the Jews." For good measure he added that "we cannot apologize for what happened until the Jews apologize first for turning their Polish neighbors over to the Soviets before the German occupation." According to Orlowski, the truth was simple. The Germans alone were to blame and Poles only helped when they were forced to.[32]

Christian nationalists, such as the right-wing parliamentarian from the Jedwabne region Michal Kaminski, echoed such arguments. They disputed the testimonies in Gross's book as being biased and incomplete. Like the Krakow-based Organization of Veterans and Independence Fighters, Kaminsiki was upset by the apology made by the Polish president.[33] At his suggestion, some Jedwabne residents formed a committee to defend the sullied reputation of their town. Clearly, for some Poles, coming to terms with the dark shadows of Jedwabne's past threatened their deepest patriotic and traditional Catholic beliefs.[34]

The primate of Poland himself, Cardinal Jozef Glemp, did not help matters either. Initially, he seemed to question whether Poles were indeed responsible for the massacre in Jedwabne, downplaying its significance by calling it "a local tragedy."[35] Glemp subsequently backtracked (following a protest letter from the rabbi of Warsaw, Michael Schudrich), conceding that "the burning of Jews, forced by Poles into a barn, is indisputable."[36] In a subsequent address Glemp compared the murders in Jedwabne to Katyn (where Polish officers were killed on Stalin's orders), Dachau, Rwanda, the Balkans and Palestine – all of them symbols which "elicit our pain as members of the human species." Not surprisingly, the Warsaw rabbi found such comparisons "demeaning to the memory of the martyrs of Jedwabne" and the amorphous analogy with recent events in Israel to be highly inappropriate. Cardinal Glemp's official statement also expressed concern about the current publication of Gross's book in English. "Today, the release of its English-language version is being awaited with anxiety, because the truth thereby revealed to Americans is expected to unleash Jewry's sharp attacks on Poles."[37]

Glemp made it clear that unlike Kwasniewski, he had no intention of visiting Jedwabne for the 60th anniversary commemoration (July 2001) and saw no cause for Polish national remorse or a feeling of collective guilt. He emphasized that "the only source of the Jews' systematic extermination had been Hitlerite totalitarianism and local animosities sometimes succumbed to that current and were used instrumentally." Glemp rejected any suggestion that "the blindness provoked in the people of Jedwabne and vicinity be extended to the entire Polish nation,' and opposed government proposals that "on such and such a day the Catholic Church should conduct major prayers in Jedwabne, repent for its sins and ask forgiveness for the genocide."[38] Instead he favored a joint Christian-Jewish religious ceremony in Warsaw that would be apolitical and would ask for "God's forgiveness for the sins that have been committed." Though Glemp evoked Rabbi Schudrich as the author of this suggestion, the Warsaw rabbi replied that a ceremony in Jedwabne was essential, observing: "Our tradition says that it is most appropriate to remember and mourn the loss that we have suffered in the place where it happened." Eventually a mass was held on 27 May 2001 at the All Saints' Church in Warsaw which passed off in a dignified manner. But Glemp subsequently managed to dampen the effect by suggesting that Jews also owed Poles an apology for their wartime collaboration with the Soviets.

Polish defensiveness over the Jedwabne massacre is apparent not only in Glemp's ambivalent remarks but in the seemingly never-ending quest for "motives" and viable explanations that might somehow mitigate its impact. But there are no silver linings in this story. Even the Wyrzkowski family who heroically saved seven Jedwabne Jews at considerable risk to their lives were obliged to hide this fact from their neighbors and were later forced to flee the region. As Gross puts it, they were seen as embarrassing witnesses to the crimes that had been committed by their fellow Poles.[39]

The Jedwabne affair certainly tarnished Poland's self-image about its exemplary heroism during the war and its romantic Messianic myth of Poland as the "Christ of the Nations." However, this does not turn Poles into co-perpetrators of the Holocaust or diminish in any way the primary German responsibility for the "Final Solution." What Jedwabne showed is that Poles (like other nations) could be both victims and perpetrators at the same time. There were "ordinary Poles" as well as "ordinary Germans" who could obey evil impulses and become "willing executioners," of their own free will. These facts, long repressed, signal the end of Polish innocence about their role in the Shoah. To their credit it should be said that many Poles have avoided the temptation to whitewash this difficult truth and have conducted their soul-searching in a dignified spirit of contrition and self-critical reflection.

Jan Gross's dispassionate, low-key, but compelling account of the atrocity at Jedwabne has performed an important service in provoking this national catharsis and encouraging a thorough cleansing of the Polish conscience. On 10 July 2001, at a solemn memorial ceremony in Jedwabne, President Kwasniewski, speaking with dignity and simplicity, recalled the horrors that had taken place sixty years earlier:

> For this crime we should beg the souls of the dead and their families for forgiveness: this is why today, as a citizen and as President of the Republic of Poland, I beg their pardon – in my

own name, and in the name of those Poles whose conscience is shattered by that crime.[40]

NOTES

1. Michael C. Steinlauf, *Bondage to the Dead: Poland and the Memory of the Holocaust* (New York: Syracuse Univ. Press, 1997) provides a good account of how this self-image evolved after 1945.
2. Jan T. Gross, *Neighbors: The Destruction of the Jewish Community in Jedwabne, Poland* (Princeton, NJ: Princeton Univ. Press, 2001), p. 19.
3. Ibid.
4. For details of the 1949 trial, see ibid., pp. 27–32.
5. See Antony Polonsky, "Beyond Condemnation, Apologetics and Apologies: On the Complexity of Polish Behavior toward the Jews during the Second World War," *Studies in Contemporary Jewish*, XIII (1997), pp. 190–224.
6. Quoted by Steven Erlanger, "Soul-Searching at Another Polish Massacre Site," *New York Times*, 19 April 2001.
7. Ibid.
8. See *Poles on Jedwabne* (Warsaw, 2001) containing a selection of articles from the Polish press and the introduction by Israel Gutman, pp. 9–16.
9. This point is amplified at greater length by Abraham Brumberg, "Murder Most Foul. Polish Responsibility for the Massacres at Jedwabne," *Times Literary Supplement*, 2 March 2001.
10. See Robert S. Wistrich, *Hitler and the Holocaust* (London, 2001), pp. 155–89.
11. See Jan Blonski, "The Poor Poles Look at the Ghetto," in A. Polonsky, ed., *My Brother's Keeper? Polish Debates on the Holocaust* (London, 1989), pp. 34–52.
12. Joanna Michlic, "The Troubling Past: Polish Collective Memory of the Holocaust. An Overview, *East European Jewish Studies* 1 (1999), pp. 79–85.
13. These are the closing words of *Neighbors*, p. 173.
14. Ibid., p. 9.
15. Tomasz Strzembosc, "Przemilczana kolabtoracja," *Rzeczpospolita* 27–28 Jan. 2001, pp. 5–6.
16. See Jan Gross, *Upiorna dekada* (Krakow, 1998), which deals with stereotypes of Jews, Poles, Germans and communists between 1939 and 1948.
17. On the historical background to this myth, see André Gerrits, "Antisemitism and Anti-Communism: They Myth of 'Judeo-

Communist' in Eastern Europe," *East European Jewish Affairs* 1 (1995), pp. 49–72.

18. M.J. Chodakiewicz, "Kłopoty z kuracją szokową," *Rzeczpospolita*, 5 Jan. 2001; for Slavomir Radon's comments, see Slawomir Majman, "Jedwabne," *The Warsaw Voice*, 4 March 2001.

19. J.R. Nowak, "Kto falszuje historie," *Nasz Dziennik*, 13–14 May 2000.

20. Leszek Czajkowski, "Jedwabny interes," *Nasza Polska*, 16 Jan. 2001

21. Leon Kalewski, "Prostujemy Klamstwa o pogromie w Jedwabne," *Nasze Polska*, 10 May 2000.

22. Chodakiewicz, "Kłopoty z kuracją szokową."

23. Zdisław Krasnodębski, "Z prawdą naz ty," *Zycie*, 11 Dec. 2000.

24. Tomasz Szarota, "Czy na pewno juz wszystko wiemy?" *Gazeta Wyborcza* 2–3 (Dec. 2000). This article was reproduced in *Poles on Jedwabne*, pp. 105–11.

25. See Jaczek Zakowski, "Kazdy sąsiad ma inię," *Gazeta Wyborcza* 18–19 Nov. 2000.

26. Joanna Tokarska-Bakir, "Obsesja niewinnosci," *Gazeta Wyborcza*, 2–3 Dec. 2000.

27. Adam Michnik, "Poles and the Jews: How Deep the Guilt?" *New York Times*, 17 March 2001.

28. On 10 July 2001, Kwasniewski's speech was broadcast live on Polish television and his apology was very explicit. See Andrzej Stylinski, Associated Press report, "Jedwabne," 10 July 2001, and "Poland's Reckoning," *Wall Street Journal*, 13 July 2001.

29. See *Jerusalem Post*, 16 May 2001.

30. Quoted by Beata Pasek, "Poles Face Truth of Jedwabne," Associated Press report, 11 March 2001.

31. Ibid.

32. Ibid.

33. Ibid.

34. R. Bender, "Trzy pytania do prof. Ryszarda Bender," *Gtos*, 25 Nov. 2000, provides an intellectual justification for this Christian nationalist backlash against Gross and his advocates.

35. Eric J. Greenberg, "Polish Church Leader Roils Jews Again," *Jewish Week*, 9 March 2001.

36. Ibid.

37. Statement by Jozef Cardinal Glemp, Roman Catholic Primate of Poland, Warsaw, 4 March 2001. Official Translation.

38. Ibid.

39. Gross, *Neighbors*, pp. 129–31.

40. "Poland Apologizes for World War II Pogrom," *Jerusalem Post*, 11 July 2001. The new inscription on the monument at Jedwabne now reads:

"In memory of the Jews of Jedwabne and surrounding areas, men, women and children, fellow-dwellers of this land, murdered and burned alive at this site on July 10, 1941. As a warning to future generations not to allow the sin of hatred spawned by German Nazism to ever again set the residents of this land against each other." It was devised before the government-led investigation officially confirmed that Poles had played a "decisive" part in the Jedwabne massacre. Polish public prosecutor Radoslaw Ignatiew finally presented the findings of his year-long investigation in July 2002. He noted that German special forces had probably incited the killings but did not actively participate in them. "We have to conclude that the role of the local population was decisive in the perpetration of this criminal act," *Jerusalem Post*, 10 July 2002.

BOOK REVIEWS AND
PUBLICATIONS RECEIVED

Book Reviews

Las Derechas: The Extreme Right in Argentina, Brazil and Chile.
By Sandra McGee Deutsch. Stanford University Press, 1999, 586 pp.

Sandra McGee Deutsch's book is a noteworthy historical analysis of the evolution and characteristics of the extreme right between 1890 and 1939, in three Latin-American countries which form the southern triangle of the continent – Argentina, Brazil and Chile. Although the extreme right in these countries has been researched in the past, this book undertakes a comparative analysis between these countries over a period of more than fifty years.

In selecting the title *Las Derechas*, a plural form in Spanish which has no English equivalent, McGee wanted to stress the heterogeneity of the extreme right. It is, indeed, a well-chosen title, since the development of the right in Latin-America reflects almost the entire spectrum of the right in Europe, from moderate, conservative and traditional rightists to radicals and fascists, with a whole range of ideological nuances in-between.

In spite of the socio-economic and demographic differences between these countries, they share much in common in terms of history, culture, religion and mentality. All three inherited a joint Ibero-American past which included, during the nineteenth century, freeing themselves from the colonial powers of Spain and Portugal, themselves culturally alike. There is also a measure of similarity in the socio-economic and political problems encountered by these three countries as they developed in the early twentieth century. Hence, the common historical-cultural background of Catholic Latin America serves the author as a methodological basis for her comparative study of the extreme right.

Three periods are reviewed: from the last decade of the 19th century until the outbreak of World War I (1890–1914); from the war until the mid-twenties; and from the end of the 1920s until 1939, when World War II began. Dividing the book into relatively short periods allowed the author to scrutinize closely the most prominent groups and organizations in each period. Taking each country separately, she carried out an in-depth examination of each period, while applying uniform parameters to the three countries, such as relations between state and religion, authoritarianism, fascism, rightist historical revisionism, populism, the right and the military forces, the right and the Catholic Church, the role of women and antisemitism. Thus, a panoramic vista has been created, made possible by a comparative approach to material over a relatively long time-span.

The primary sources of the research are extensive; a variety of archives in these three countries and in the United States, and a wealth of secondary sources buttress her assertions.

The author pays considerable attention to ideology, stressing correctly that the right is not merely a reaction to the left, but has its own ideological position. In Latin America the influence of medieval philosophers such as Thomas Aquinas is still felt, as well as that of modern European political theorists of extreme nationalism, such as French rightists Charles Maurras and Maurice Barrès, and Spanish Integrists and *Tradicionalistas*.

When dealing with the worldview of Latin American ultra-rightists, McGee Deutsch, in contrast to other historians of Latin America, finds antisemitism of great significance, especially in Argentina. The forms which antisemitism takes in each of these countries were dealt with, each under a separate heading, and examined closely for their place in the philosophy of the rightists in each country. Thus, we learn both of the European sources of antisemitism, and its local formulation and political context. Antisemitic views began to flourish amongst rightists at the beginning of the century, constituting an important element in their worldview by the 1920s, before the advent of Hitler. Even prior to the period of the persecution of the Jews in Europe, the Jews of Latin America had felt the destructive force of modern European antisemitism, which conformed well with traditional religious stereotypes, and intensified in the 1930s.

This important and probing work by Sandra McGee Deutsch is of value to researchers of Latin America and to the general reader as well, particularly Latin American Jewry.

Dr. Graciela Ben-Dror
Stephen Roth Institute,
Oranim Academic College,
and University of Haifa

Antisemitism in Slovak Politics (1989-1999). By Pavol Mestan. Museum of Jewish Culture, Bratislava, and Tel Aviv University, 2000, 287 pp.

Professor Pavol Mestan, founder and director of the Museum of Jewish Culture, Bratislava, has written an original, comprehensive work, which summarizes the nature of antisemitism in the nationalist movements and the press of post-communist Slovakia. The study focuses chiefly on the period after the partition of Czechoslovakia in January 1993 into two independent states, the Czech Republic and Slovakia.

The small Jewish population, 3,000 Jews in a population of about 5.5 million, would not seem to warrant antisemitic activity. The majority are elderly, survivors of the Shoah, with a minority born after the war. They are not prominent in government, in economic life, or even in local liberal movements. A very small number have entered academic life and the liberal professions and take part in local community activity. What, then, accounts for the sometimes obsessive presence of antisemitism in Slovakian public life that is well documented in this volume? Is it unique and thus in essence unlike antisemitism in the rest of central and eastern Europe since the fall of communism?

Mestan clearly indicates the special nature of Slovak antisemitism in the post-communist period, unfolding a wide canvas that depicts the deep roots of antisemitism in the distant and recent past. He distinguishes three sources which contribute to the development of this phenomenon: a religious basis, cultivated by senior Slovakian clerical officials at the end of the 19th century; a nationalist element, particularly the call of the Catholic priest Josef Tiso, an ally of Hitler, to cleanse Slovakia of its "eternal enemy" the Jews; and the antisemitism of the communist period, during which antisemitism was coupled with anti-Zionism.

Tiso came to power as president of the Nazi-protected "independent" Slovakia in 1939. He continued to carry out his anti-Jewish policies until the end of the war, when he was tried for his crimes against the Jews and his alliance with Hitler, found guilty and hanged in 1946.

As head of state, Tiso was responsible for the destruction of Slovakian Jewry and for the dispatch of the Jews to the death camps in Poland, in March 1942, without pressure from Nazi Germany and in defiance of the Vatican's request to prevent this. Further, Tiso's government promised to pay the Germans 500 Reich Marks for every Jew deported. This was the first instance in the history of the Shoah in which a government that called itself "independent" actually paid the Germans for the deportation of Jews. The deportations, which ceased in October 1942, were renewed in fall 1944. An estimated 100,000 Slovakian Jews (including from territories annexed by Hungary) were murdered in the Shoah.

Antisemitism was twinned with anti-Zionism during the communist period under the influence of Soviet ideology, particularly toward the end of Stalin's life. The Slánský Trial (the show trial of Jewish Czechoslovak Party Secretary General Rudolf Slánský and his alleged accomplices) marked the culmination of accusations of treason against the Jews. Of the fourteen convicted of treason and sentenced to death in the 1952–53 trials, eleven were Jews. Even after Stalin's death, Soviet propaganda throughout the Soviet bloc portrayed the Zionist movement and its membership as "war mongers" and collaborators with the American imperialists.

In the post-communist period, as Slovakia moved toward democratization, one might have expected that antisemitism would disappear completely. Instead, the old-new Slovakian antisemitism took on a special character – the focus of Mestan's research – as the Slovakian nationalist movement strove to glorify the image of Tiso as the founder of Slovak independence and the father of modern Slovakia. In their attempt to rehabilitate him, they disregarded completely his responsibility for the extermination of Slovak Jews and his pact with Hitler. Thus, a longstanding confrontation resulted, between the nationalist movement which favored restoring the memory of Tiso and the liberal movement and Jewish congregational leaders who strenuously opposed it. This confrontation gives Slovakian antisemitism its distinguishing feature, whereby the public debate focuses perhaps more on Tiso's crimes against the Jews than on his role as Hitler's ally, and in particular, on the suppression of the anti-fascist revolt in Slovakia in August 1944.

While this conflict seems unique, it is, in fact, rather similar to the situation in Romania, where the nationalist parties seek to glorify Ion Antonescu, fascist leader of Romania from 1941 to 1944. Antonescu ordered the mass slaughter of Jews from Bessarabia and northern Bukovino when the German and Romanian armies attacked the USSR in June 1941, and shortly thereafter ruthlessly sent all the survivors to ghettos and camps in Transnistria, where about 90,000 Jews were killed, without any pressure from Germany.

The reaction of the Slovak governments, like that of collaborationist regimes such as Romania, is a measure of its ability to cut itself off from its fascist past, and to admit the crimes committed by those regimes against the Jews, against liberals and against humanity. The Slovakian government has repeatedly declared its dissociation from the "independent" Slovakian state under Nazi protection since the revelation of documentation connected with Tiso's crimes. Mestan is correct in his belief that informing the Slovak people, especially the generation born after the war, of the destruction of the Jews native to the country by the country's fascist leaders would reduce the nationalists' prospects of clearing Tiso's name and win their acceptance as symbols of the struggle for independence. Education is of prime importance, but legal and organizational tools should also be employed to stop antisemitsm: there must be appropriate legislation and enforcement tools to carry it out.

The attitude of the Slovak governments toward rehabilitation and toward the Shoah in general is encouraging. In any event, it serves the national interest, whether it is to further integration into the European Union or to improve the country's image in the future. Israel, too, should play an active role. While it cannot interfere in domestic affairs, it can, and should, extend all possible help in revealing the historical facts, in order to curb antisemitism. Mestan's research proves how vital this is. The book is important not only as a rich source for scholars and those interested in antisemitism in modern Slovakia but as a source of practical ideas about how to limit it.

Dr. Joseph Govrin
Non-resident ambassador in
Slovakia while ambassador to
Austria (1993–95), and the
author of several studies
on Eastern and Central
Europe

The Catholic Church and the Jews: Argentina 1933–1945 (Hebrew). By Graciela Ben-Dror. Zalman Shazar Center, Historical Society of Israel and Vidal Sassoon Center for the Study of Antisemitism, Jerusalem, 2000, 320 pp.

This book, based on the author's doctoral thesis completed at the Institute of Contemporary Jewry of the Hebrew University of Jerusalem in 1993, is an innovation in several respects. Ben-Dror first deals with the changes in the Catholic Church which had an impact on the Jews, against the socio-political and ideological background of Argentina from

1933 to 1945. She then analyzes the attitude of the Catholic Church toward Nazism and the Holocaust against the backdrop of developments in the international arena during those years. Her original research in this section is compelling.

The author reviews the doctrinaire approach and the literature of leading antisemitic authors, especially Julio Meinvielle and Hugo Wast, as representative trends within the Church (Chapter 2), and as part of the nationalistic and integrist project of re-Christianizing Argentinean society. Ben-Dror then analyzes ecclesiastical documents and catechismal educational materials of the Church hierarchy in relation to Jews and Judaism, as well as the ideology and deeds of several antisemitic priests. She proceeds to the period from the military putsch of 4 June 1943, which she labels "Catholic Argentina" because of the alliance of the Church with the armed forces. During this period, 1943–45, the Jews, according to Ben-Dror, suffered state antisemitism as a result of Catholic integrist influence among senior officials. The Church itself did not interfere, nor did it try to attenuate or condemn anti-Jewish manifestations, whether they emanated from laymen or members of the clergy (Chapter 4).

Ben-Dror's concludes in this section of the book that the integrist Catholic trend that strove to re-Christianize Argentinean society increased its hegemony over the hierarchy and over many clergymen, as well as over nationalist laymen and the armed forces. She also determines that the integrist theological doctrine, which tended to exclude anyone who was not Catholic from Argentinean society, and first and foremost the Jews, became an alternative ideology, that was powerful enough to challenge the secular, liberal, pluralistic society which Argentina had known until 1943. Similar conclusions have been reached in studies on Argentinean nationalism and Catholicism, most recently in the work of Loris Zanatta (1996). The latter's work provides another perspective: portrayal of the Argentinean Church as part of the universal and hierarchical Church, and as subordinate to the Vatican. Ben Dror detects neither antisemitism nor philosemitism in official documents and pastoral letters handed down by the Argentinean bishopric during the period 1933–45. Nevertheless, a great deal of antisemitism appears in publications of the lower ranks of the clergy, including parochial weeklies and Catholic newspapers.

The second section analyzes the official position of the Church toward events in Europe, before and during World War II: the Nazi regime and its ideology, the papal encyclicals on Nazism and communism, the question of Jewish refugees, the outbreak of war, the reaction to the German invasion of Poland, the Molotov-Ribbentrop Pact, the conquest of the Soviet Union, and Argentinean neutrality during the war. Ben-Dror proceeds to examine the Church's stand on the violence perpetrated against the Jews during the first stages of the war, and then after the implementation of the "Final Solution," in the territories under Nazi German occupation (Chapters 8 and 9). The last chapter deals with the postwar attitude of the Church to the beginning of democratization in Argentina and of Argentinean Catholics toward this process.

Despite the fact that official documents issued by senior Church officials did not reflect anti-Jewish positions, the author's interpretation of the silence of the Argentinean Church toward Jewish suffering during the Holocaust is a historiographic innovation. The lack of response is exemplified in the complete inaction of the Archbishop of Buenos Aires when requested by German bishops at a meeting in Rome in early 1939 to urge the Argentinean authorities to permit entry into the country of "Aryan Catholics" (Jews who had converted and been baptized). This was in contrast to the case of Brazil.

The author concludes that while Church documents and publications evidenced doctrinaire anti-communist and anti-liberal positions, integrist antisemitism was not apparent, although it was latent in the discourse of the Church hierarchy. It was not discussed openly because respect for Jews and Judaism was an integral part of theological thought. Nevertheless, unofficial Catholic publications such as *Criterio* and *El Pueblo*, analyzed by the author, expressed uncensored Judeophobia, which included both traditional and new motifs.

Methodologically, this work belongs to historical studies that view the Holocaust as a unique phenomenon which must be understood on a global scale, especially in respect to a worldwide institution such as the Catholic Church. The author uses a comparative approach when considering the Vatican position and that of the Argentinean "Romanized" hierarchy toward Nazism, the war and the Holocaust. This section of the book is based on an exhaustive analysis of official Church documents as well as on unofficial Catholic publications.

Nevertheless, in such an important study of Catholic antisemitism it would have been interesting to include a comparison with Protestantism (a chapter that appeared in the author's Ph.D. dissertation). Further, an examination of hatred of other "enemies" of the radical Catholic right, such as communists, the proletarian movement and the secular and liberal modernist movement, would have been useful. A possible direction for further research is investigating the indistinct border between the radical extra-parliamentary right and the conservative parliamentary right in Argentina, as well as the implications for the Jews of political practices of leading forces of Catholic fascist movements.

As to primary ecclesiastical sources, the author studied systematically and for the first time important official publications of the archbishops of Buenos Aires and Cordoba, in order to bring to light their image of the Jews. She also analyzed the documents of Catholic Action, a lay Catholic institution, and more than 60 weekly publications from different parishes of Buenos Aires and other cities around the country. Until the publication of Ben Dror's book knowledge of Catholic antisemitism was based on studies of the nationalist Catholic movement. Thanks to her research, it has been enriched by various ecclesiastical sources.

Leonardo Senkman
Hebrew University of
Jerusalem

In Brief

"The Plunder of Jewish Property during the Holocaust" – *Confronting European History.* Edited by Avi Beker. Basingstoke, Hampshire: Palgrave, 2001, 355 pp.

This is a timely publication. The articles describe both the plunder of Jewish property during the Holocaust and the situation of reparations today. After presenting a general framework – myths about Jewish wealth, legal aspects and the confrontation with history – the author examines eastern Europe and then western Europe (Switzerland, France, Britain, Norway, Austria, Spain, Portugal, Belgium, Italy and the Netherlands). The extent of the plunder is upsetting, but there is encouragement in Dr. Beker's contention that the question of reparations has driven the European countries to do some soul searching regarding their national historical account during World War II; and that this process will benefit their international relations, and perhaps their attitude toward the Jewish people. The book is well produced and constitutes a major contribution to a central contemporary issue.

The Popes against the Jews: The Vatican's Role in the Rise of Modern Anti-Semitism. By David I. Kertzer. New York: Alfred A. Knopf, 2001, 355 pp.

David Kertzer's book deals with the role of the Church and its impact on the emergence of modern antisemitism and the Holocaust. The author describes one hundred years of accumulating hatred and demonization of Jews in Europe, detailing such phenomena as forced baptisms; the pontifical act of Pope Leo XII in 1823, which led to the incarceration of the Jews in ghettos "in order to overcome the evil consequences of freedom"; hostile propaganda against the Jews in the Catholic press; the allegation of Jewish ritual murder; and Pope Pius XII's conduct during World War II. Kertzer proves that the Vatican Commission's document, "We Remember: A Reflection on the Shoah," published in 1998, does not constitute an apology for the Holocaust, since it differentiates between anti-Judaism and antisemitism. While anti-Judaism, meaning religiously- and socially-based hatred of the Jews, typified the Church's attitude to the Jews, Nazi antisemitism, which derived from race theories, was firmly rejected by the Church. In Kertzer's opinion this distinction allowed the Roman Catholic Church to absolve itself of any responsibility for the spread of hatred toward the Jews, thus paving the way for the Holocaust.

Muslim Anti-Semitism. A Clear and Present Danger. By Robert S. Wistrich. New York: The American Jewish Committee, 2002, 57 pp.

Antisemitism penetrated the Arab and Muslim worlds at the end of the 19th century and became more widespread with the outbreak of the Arab-Israeli conflict. The cultural and ideological origins of this antisemitism and the assessment of its danger are contentious issues among scholars researching the subject. Triggered by the events of 11 September 2001, Wistrich's concise booklet *Muslim Anti-Semitism* tries to provide a clear-cut answer to these questions. Surveying the development of Arab/Islamic antisemitism and the major themes characterizing it, the study cites and disputes some basic assumptions. This thought-provoking publication is intended to sound "an alarm bell for a very clear and immediate threat to Jews worldwide."

Aus Dem Schatten, Der Katastrophe, Die Deutsch-Israelischen Beziehungen In Dear Ära Konrad Adenauer und David Ben-Gurion. By Niels Hansen. Düsseldorf, 2002, pp. 891 pp.

Written by Germany's ambassador to Israel in the 1980s, this lengthy study examines the development of Israeli–West German relations from the end of the 1940s until 1965, when diplomatic ties between the two countries were officially established. The study focuses mainly on the role of Israel's first Prime Minister David Ben-Gurion and first West German Chancellor Konrad Adenauer in creating a special relationship between the two countries. The topics discussed include the evolution of direct negotiations on the question of reparations, and encompassing the public and political debates in both countries; the arms agreements between the two countries and their political implications for Israel; and the impact of Israeli-German negotiations on relations between West Germany and the Arab countries, notably Egypt. Also dealt with are the problematic issues of former Nazis who held senior positions in the Adenauer administration and antisemitism in West Germany at the end of the 1950s and early 1960s. The research is based on documents found in Israeli and German archives.

Publications Received

Almeras, Philippe, *Je suis le bouc: Celine et l'antisemitisme*. Paris: Denoël, 2000.

Aull-Furstenberg, Margret, *Lebensluge Hitler-Jugend: aus dem Tagebuch eines BDM-Mädchens*. Wien: Ueberreuter, 2001.

Beker, Avi (ed.), *The Plunder of Jewish Property during the Holocaust. Confronting European History*. Houndmills, UK: Palgrave, 2001.

Ben-Dor, David, *Die schwarze Mütze: Geschichte eines Mitschuldigen*. Leipzig: Reclam, 2000.

Benz, Wolfgang, *Geschichte des Dritten Reiches*. München: C.H. Beck, 2000.

Berschel, Holger, *Bürokratie und Terror: das Judenreferat der Gestapo Dusseldorf 1935–1945*. Essen: Klartext, 2001.

Bonnett, Alastair, *Anti-racism*. London: Routledge, 2000.

Burrin, Philippe, *Fascisme, nazisme, autoritarisme*. Paris: Editions du Seuil, 2000.

Burrows, Stephanie, *Tucholsky and France*. Leeds: Maney Pub. for the Modern Humanities Research Association and the Institute of Germanic Studies, University of London School of Advanced Study, 2001.

Dean, Martin, *Collaboration in the Holocaust: Crimes of the Local Police in Belorussia and Ukraine, 1941–44*. New York: St. Martin's Press, 2000.

Dierker, Wolfgang, *Himmlers Glaubenskrieger: der Sicherheitsdienst der SS und seine Religionspolitik, 1933-1941*. Paderborn: F. Schoningh, 2002.

Dorr, Thomas, *"Mühsam und so weiter, was waren das fur Namen": Zeitgeist und Zynismus im nationalistisch-antisemitischen Werk des Graphikers A. Paul Weber*. Lübeck: Erich-Muhsam-Gesellschaft, 2000.

Dutlinger, Anne D. (ed.), *Art, Music, and Education as Strategies for Survival: Theresienstadt, 1941–45*. New York: Herodias, 2001.

Frederiksen, Elke P. & Wallach, Martha Kaarsberg (eds.), *Facing Fascism and Confronting the Past: German Women Writers from Weimar to the Present*. Albany, NY: State University of New York Press, 2000.

Gastfriend, Edward, *My Father's Testament: Memoir of a Jewish Teenager, 1938–1945*. Philadelphia: Temple University Press, 2000.

Goggin, James E. and Goggin, Eileen Brockman, *Death of a "Jewish Science": Psychoanalysis in the Third Reich*. West Lafayette, Ind.: Purdue University Press, 2001.

Grewenig, von Adi & Jager, Margret, *Medien in Konflikten: Holocaust, Krieg, Ausgrenzung*. Duisburg: Duisburger Institut für Sprach und Sozialforschung, 2000.

Hafner, Georg M. & Schapira, Esther, *Die Akte Alois Brunner: warum einer der grössten Naziverbrecher noch immer auf freiem Fuss ist.* Frankfurt: Campus, 2000.

Har-El, Moshe, *"Ich habe nicht gewusst, dass wir noch schlimmere Zeit vor uns hatten": von Mahrisch-Ostrau in die Berge der Tatra und nach Israel.* Konstanz: Labhard, 2001

Heyken, Eberhard, *Die deutsch-ukrainischen Beziehungen: gestern, heute und morgen auf dem Weg nach Europa.* Konstanz: Hartung-Gorre, 2001

Honigsman, Jakob, *Juden in der Westukraine: jüdisches Leben und Leiden in Ostgalizien, Wolhynien, der Bukowina und Transkarpatien, 1933–1945.* Konstanz : Hartung-Gorre, 2000.

IBOPE, *Knowledge and Remembrance of the Holocaust in Brazil: A Public-Opinion Survey Conducted for the American Jewish Committee, Sao Paulo, March 22–25, 2001.* New York: The American Jewish Committee, 2001.

Kallis, Aristotle A., *Fascist Ideology: Territory and Expansionism in Italy and Germany, 1922–1945.* London: Routledge, 2000.

Klein, Gerda Weissmann & Klein, Kurt, *The Hours After: Letters of Love and Longing in War's Aftermath.* New York: St. Martin's Press, 2000.

Koehl, Robert Lewis, *The SS: A History, 1919–45.* Stroud, Glocestershire: Tempus, 2000.

Kohler, Joachim, *Wagner's Hitler: The Prophet and His Disciple.* Oxford: Blackwell, 2001.

Kotek, Joel & Rigoulot, Pierre, *Le siècle des camps: detention, concentration, extermination: cent ans de mal radical.* Paris: J.C. Lattes, 2000.

Laqueur, Walter (ed.), *The Holocaust Encyclopedia.* New Haven: Yale University Press, 2001.

Le Groignec, Jacques, *Pétain face a l'histoire.* Paris: Nouvelles editions latines, 2000.

Linck, Stephan, *Der Ordnung verpflichtet: Deutsche Polizei, 1933–1949: der Fall Flensburg.* Paderborn: F. Schoningh, 2000.

Maser, Werner, *Hermann Göring: Hitlers janusköpfiger Paladin: die politische Biographie.* Berlin: Edition q., 2000.

Meyer, Michel, *Le demon est-il allemand?.* Paris: B. Grasset, 2000.

Morgan, Michael L. (ed.), *A Holocaust Reader: Responses to the Nazi Extermination.* New York: Oxford University Press, 2001.

Naake, Erhard, *Nietzsche und Weimar: Werk und Wirkung im 20. Jahrhundert.* Koln: Bohlau, 2000.

Niewyk, Donald L. & Nicosia, Francis, *The Columbia Guide to the Holocaust.* New York: Columbia University Press, 2000.

Nordbruch, Goetz, *The Socio-Historical Background of Holocaust Denial in Arab Countries: Reactions to Roger Garaudy's* The Founding Myths of Israeli Politics. Jerusalem: Vidal Sassoon International Center for the Study of Antisemitism, 2001.

La persécution des Juifs de France 1940–1944 et le retablissement de la légalité republicaine: Recueil des textes officiels 1940–1999. Paris: Documentation francaise, 2000.

Pfau, Dieter, *Christenkreuz und Hakenkreuz: Siegen und das Siegerland am Vorabend des "Dritten Reiches"* Bielefeld: Verlag für Regionalgeschichte, 2001.

Polonsky, Antony (ed.), *Focusing on the Holocaust and its Aftermath.* London: Littman Library of Jewish Civilization, 2000.

Post im Schatten des Hakenkreuzes: das Schicksal der jüdischen Familie Sternberg in ihren Briefen von Berlin nach Tokyo in der Zeit von 1910 bis 1950. Berlin: Duncker & Humblot, 2000.

Prost , Antoine, Rémi Skoutelsky & Sonia Etienne, *Aryanisation economique et restitutions.* Paris: La Documentation francaise, 2000.

Raulet, Gerard, *Historismus, Sonderweg und dritte Wege.* Frankfurt am Main: P. Lang, 2001.

Roegele, Otto Bernhard, *Gestapo gegen Schuler: Die Gruppe "Christopher" in Bruchsal.* Konstanz: Universitätsverlag, 2000.

Romberg, Otto R., *Jews in Germany after 1945: Citizens or "Fellow" Citizens?.* Frankfurt: Tribune, 2000.

Roth, John K., *Holocaust Politics.* Louisville, KY: Westminster John Knox Press, 2001.

Roth, John K. and Maxwell-Meynard, Elisabeth, *Remembering for the Future: The Holocaust in an Age of Genocides.* New York: Palgrave, 2001.

Rusu, Victor, *Damals im Schtetl: jüdisches Leben in Rumanien: erlebte und belieferte Geschichten.* Konstanz: Hartung-Gorre, 2001.

Sarfati, Georges Elia, *Le Vatican et la Shoah, ou comment l'Eglise s'absout de son passé: analyse du "Document de l'Eglise de Rome sur la Shoah."* Paris: Berg International, 2000.

Schenk, Dieter, *Hitlers Mann in Danzig: Albert Forster und die NS-Verbrechen in Danzig-Westpreussen.* Bonn: J.H.W. Dietz, 2000.

Schneider, Richard Chaim, *Wir sind da!: die Geschichte der Juden in Deutschland von 1945 bis heute.* Berlin: Ullstein, 2000.

Schultze, Winfried & Oexle, Otto Gerhard, *Deutsche Historiker im Nationalsozialismus.* Frankfurt: Fischer Taschenbuch, 1999.

Seidler, Victor Jeleniewski, *Shadows of the Shoah: Jewish Identity and Belonging.* Oxford: Berg, 2000,

Smelser, Ronald, *Die SS: Elite unter dem Totenkopf: 30 Lebensläufe.* Paderborn: F. Schoningh, 2000.

Spector, Shmuel and Wigoder, Geoffrey (eds.), *The Encyclopedia of Jewish Life before and during the Holocaust.* New York: New York University Press, 2001.

Stolle, Michael, *Die Geheime Staatspolizei in Baden: Personal, Organisation, Wirkung und Nachwirken einer regionalen Verfolgungsbehörde im Dritten.* Konstanz: UVK, 2001

Thatcher, Nicole, *A Literary Analysis of Charlotte Delbo's Concentration Camp Representation.* Lewiston: E. Mellen, 2000.

Verolme, Hetty E., *The Children's House of Belsen.* Fremantle, Western Australia: Fremantle Arts Centre Press, 2000.

Wachs, Philipp-Christian, *Der Fall Theodor Oberlander (1905–1998): Ein Lehrstück deutscher Geschichte.* Frankfurt: Campus, 2000.

Wenck, Alexandra-Eileen, *Zwischen Menschenhandel und "Endlösung": Das Konzentrationslager Bergen-Belsen.* Paderborn: F. Schoningh, 2000.

Wiehn, Erhard Roy (ed.), *Babij Jar 1941: Das Massaker deutscher Exekutionskommandos an der jüdischen Bevölkerung von Kiew , 60 Jahre danach zum Gedenken.* Konstanz: Hartung-Gorre, 2001.

Die Weimarer Republik, 1918–1933. Darmstadt: Wissenschaftliche Buchgesellschaft, 2002.

Wistrich, Robert Solomon, *Hitler and the Holocaust.* New York: Modern Library, 2001.

Zahlten, Richard, *Dr. Johanna Geissmar: von Mannheim nach Heidelberg und über den Schwarzwald durch Gurs nach Auschwitz-Birkenau, 1877–1942: Einer jüdischen Arztin 60 Jahre danach zum Gedenken.* Konstanz: Hartung-Gorre, 2001.

GENERAL ANALYSIS

Overview

The term 'the new antisemitism' refers to the current wave, which has swept much of the world since October 2000. It has been characterized as 'political antisemitism', on the one hand, because of its use by radical Islamists in their geo-political struggle against the West and its alleged spearhead the Jewish people and its state; and on the other, because of the association made in the media and by public figures between Israel and the Jewish people as an inseparable entity. In parallel, the barriers between antisemitism and anti-Zionism have been lifted and the two merged.

This definition is pertinent to two major events, both of which took place in September 2001 and made this year unique in terms of world public opinion and antisemitic activity. They were the UN World Conference against Racism (in Durban, South Africa), which ended on 9 September, and the destruction of the World Trade Center in New York, barely two days later.

The Durban conference, originally assembled to address acute world problems of discrimination, xenophobia and intolerance, was transformed into a wholesale attack on Israel and the Jewish people. During street parades, demonstrators carried banners equating Zionism with all evil, and in particular, racism and apartheid. *The Protocols of the Elders of Zion*, *Mein Kampf* and similar materials depicting modern blood libels and abhorrent images of Jews were distributed freely, and Jewish NGO delegates were physically threatened. Other factors which led to the highjacking of the conference by Arab and Muslim countries and the targeting of Israel were personal ambitions of UN officials; the Islamization of UN institutions due to the large numbers and constant pressure of Arab and Muslim states; the US and the European Union's wish to circumvent the demands presented to them to compensate former colonies and slaves with enormous sums; deep-seated anti-American sentiments prevailing in many Third World Countries as well as European ones; and the unspoken wish to shake off the burdensome shadow of the Holocaust by accusing the Jews of supporting the worst crimes. These are circumstantial factors. Yet the aggressive attacks directed solely at Israel and the Jews, and the complete disregard of other countries where human rights violations are known to be sky-rocketing, clearly point to deep-rooted and hostile emotions against an image which allegedly explains all that is evil.

However, once the Third World delegations realized the conference was serving Arab and Muslim interests alone, the tide turned and in the closing sessions a more balanced concluding document was drawn up and approved. But what was done could not be undone. Extensive media coverage transmitted the hostile atmosphere and the cynical political manipulations into millions of homes worldwide, and the immediate result was a wave of antisemitic manifestations and violence. The September 11 events enhanced this wave, with some accusing the Jews and Israel of perpetrating the attacks, thus reinforcing the image of the unscrupulous murderous Jew, the source of the world's troubles. Others blamed the attacks on US support for Israel, due to Jewish control of the government, underpinning the assumption that the Jews are indeed the source of world unrest (see below).

Worldwide processes also served as fertile ground for an increase in antisemitic manifestations: Globalization of the world economy is often identified with the Jews, because of their alleged wealth and cosmopolitan connections. The migration to the 'rich north' of refugees, asylum seekers and foreign workers has sharpened problems of national, ethnic and racial identity, and led to calls for more restrictive legislation and domestic policy. In parallel, hundreds of human rights organizations worldwide – initially established during the last decade to offer aid and advice to the disadvantaged – were persuaded to support the Palestinian cause because of generous Arab funding, a traditional empathy for the current underdog, loose and vague definitions of racism and its offspring, and the fact that Israel as a democratic state could be morally condemned, thus avoiding a confrontation with despotic Muslim regimes. Moreover, determined demands, put forward by Jewish organizations, to have the Jewish people compensated for its property looted during the Holocaust, generated resentment, since the majority of Jews now reside in wealthy countries, while millions suffer from poverty and human rights abuses.

This permissive mood, which prevailed both prior to September 2001 and afterwards, set the stage for a wave of antisemitic violence. About 50 major attacks (involving the use of weapons), and about 180 other violent incidents, were perpetrated against Jews in 2001, particularly after 11 September (and mainly by Muslims) – a total of 230, compared with 255 in 2000. France witnessed a decrease in major violent incidents and attacks, from 54 incidents in 2000 to 27 in 2001, although there were numerous other antisemitic incidents such as threats, insults and minor acts of vandalism. In the UK the numbers remained similar (39 in 2001 versus 36 in 2000), while Russia experienced a sharp increase in criminal, including antisemitic, activity in general (28 violent antisemitic incidents in 2001 compared with 6 in 2000).

Numbers are not the only indication. In 2001 there was a higher degree of violence and even vindictiveness, especially against individuals who were obviously Jewish, and against synagogues – 133 such attacks, mainly arson. This number marks a dramatic change from 1998-9, when half of violent attacks were perpetrated against cemeteries, while synagogues comprised only 20 percent. In 2000/1, attacks against individuals and synagogues made up more than half of cases. (The manifold numbers of threats, insults and calls to kill Jews, in public speeches and in demonstrations, in the media and on the Internet, were not included in the numbers presented here because of the difficulties in counting them and because of different monitoring systems in the various countries.)

Differences of opinion regarding the categorization of violence produced different estimations: in France, for instance, the authorities claimed there were 29 cases in 2001, defining them as criminal, not antisemitic, while CRIF (Conseil Representatif des Institutions Juives de France) put the number at 320 violent antisemitic incidents, and SOS Racisme, at 400 (the latter two between October 2000 and February 2002).

The prevailing political climate is a determining factor regarding violence against Jews. Following previous antisemitic events, there was an outburst of public indignation; since October 2000 the French authorities have been slow to react and have advised the Jewish community to remain quiet and inconspicuous.

It thus might be concluded that despite slightly lower numbers in 2001 compared with 2000, the level of violence continued to be high and threatening. Offensive references to Jews that had been confined to the fringes since World War II were made in European salons and among the higher echelons of society and government. Coupled with violent attacks, this development led to the dissemination of antisemitic stereotypes and to openly questioning the legitimacy of the State of Israel and even of the Jewish people. While Jewish communities perhaps pay a price for the Middle East conflict, Israel pays for the image of the Jew: "In polite company", wrote a London *Sunday Times* observer, "one uses 'Israel' when hesitating to use the word 'Jew'."

Blaming Israel and the Jews:
Antisemitic Images in the Aftermath of 11 September

The September 11 attacks on the World Trade Center (WTC) in New York and the Pentagon in Washington sent shock waves throughout the world. Alongside widespread condemnation and expressions of horror and sympathy, anti-Americanism – specifically, anger against America's "imperialist" policies and US support for Israel – was reported in various parts of the world. For antisemites – both rightists and leftists, as well as Islamists and commentators in the Arab world – the Jew was the indirect or even the direct culprit, and the antisemitic terminology of these groups was frequently similar.

After 11 September, antisemitism was expressed either in blaming the US for its support of Israel, or in directly implicating Israel in the attacks. Some antisemites claimed that US support for Israel, induced by alleged Jewish control of the US government and media, was the main motive for the Islamist terrorists' acts. The second claim, accusing Israel, particularly the Mossad and American Jews, of the attacks themselves, was a continuation of the anti-Israel and antisemitic campaign carried out in Durban, which aimed at portraying Israel and the Jews as the ultimate evil, and the main obstacle to peace between nations and religions.

Simultaneously, a wave of racist attacks on Arabs and other ethnic minorities in the US and in Western Europe erupted after the events of 11 September.

THE FIRST APPROACH: AMERICAN POLICY AS A JEWISH PLOT
The concept of US support for Israel as the main motivation of the perpetrators was propagated by extremists and antisemitic groups, as well as by Israel's opponents worldwide. For many, both on the left and the right, this concept was part of strong anti-American feelings, and the attacks were portrayed in various parts of the world as a just reaction against oppressive US policy. This explanation for the horror could not be accepted by American white supremacists. For them, it was not the American people but the Jews and their supporters in the government who were to blame. The Americans, according to white supremacist thinking, were "human shields for Israel."

The Islamist and Arab Reaction

Unlike the unequivocal horror and denunciation expressed by most nations, the reaction of the Arab world was confused and hesitant, ranging from half-hearted condemnation to sheer jubilation. This response reflected not only conflicting Arab attitudes and sentiments toward the US, but a deep-seated, centuries-old enmity between two competing powers and civilizations – Islam and the West. This hostility, exacerbated by a continued sense of humiliation experienced by the world of Islam in the last two centuries, and nourished by Usama bin Ladin's Islamist worldview, was evidently the driving force behind the attacks. Hostility toward the Jews and Israel was part and parcel of this vision. Hence, the Arab reaction to the September 11 events was composed of two interrelated positions – anti-Americanism and antisemitism.

In most Arabs states the attacks were described as the most terrifying and abominable terrorist event in US history, and were condemned for having harmed innocent civilians. Yet, instead of discussing the terrorist phenomenon emanating from within and offering explanations for the doctrines justifying it, the debate in the Arab world concentrated on the reasons for such profound anti-Americanism. Thus, most criticism of the attacks differentiated between the suffering of individual Americans and the "legitimate" damage done to the symbol of American might, and blamed US policies and America itself for the attacks. Lebanese writer George Hawi explicitly stated in the pro-Syrian paper *al-Safir* that rejecting terrorism meant disagreement with the tactics but not with the goals.

"Traditionally biased" US policy toward Israel was given as the prime reason for the deep-seated hatred of the US. Islamist groups in the Arab world and outside it also blamed the attacks on US Middle East policy, which had created over the years a series of grievances, among which support for Israel was only one. These included perceived US animosity toward Islam, US exploitation of Arab resources, American support of undemocratic regimes in the region, and US actions against Iraq. The American public, it was argued, had been misled by Israeli/Zionist domination over the American media and by the strong influence of the Jewish lobby in the US; thus, it was indifferent to the Palestinians' suffering and to Israeli aggression against them.

`Ali `Aqla `Arsan, chairman of the Syrian Arab Writers Association, admitted that when he saw the masses fleeing in horror in the streets of New York and Washington, he felt that he was being "carried in the air above the corpse of the mythological symbol of arrogant American imperialist power, whose administration had prevented the people from knowing the crimes it was committing." Some Arab commentators called on "the arch Satan," America, to reflect on why it was "the object of all that violence and antipathy," and adopt "more humane policies, less biased in favor of aggressors and occupiers."

In many Arab countries, such as Lebanon and Saudi Arabia, as well as the Palestinian Authority (PA), there were spontaneous outbursts of joy – people poured into the streets, distributed sweets to passers-by, chanted slogans of "God is Great," honked horns, flashed the victory sign and fired shots into the air. "This is the language that the United States understands"; "Let America have a taste of what we've tasted"; "The myth of America was destroyed with the WTC in New York… It is the prestige, arrogance and institutions of America that burn"; and "The super-terrorist had a taste of its own bitter medicine" – were all themes that recurred in the media. In an open letter in the Gaza Hamas mouthpiece *al-Risala*, Palestinian `Attallah Abu al-Subh wrote: "We [the Arabs] stand in line and beg Allah to let you [the Americans] drink from the cup of humiliation – and behold, heaven has answered."

Arab leaders, however, downplayed these manifestations of exaltation. Fearing American reprisals in the war against terrorism, they condemned the attacks and absolved themselves of responsibility, while simultaneously trying to appease domestic public opinion by implicitly criticizing American policy, and claiming that it bred a sense of injustice and disappointment among Arabs and Muslims. Most revealing was PA Chairman Yasir Arafat's reaction to the televised coverage of the celebrations in the PA. He banned celebratory demonstrations and warned against filming them. The PA semi-official paper *al-Hayat al-Jadida* even accused cameramen of falsifying the scenes. The only Arab leader who openly celebrated the attacks was Iraq's Saddam Husayn. He asserted that the US had reaped "the thorns that its rulers have planted in the world."

Latin America
Harsh anti-Americanism, alongside expressions of grief, was also manifested in Latin America. It reflected the deep hostility of many Latin Americans, both on the left and the right, toward what they perceived as American imperialist policies. Immediately after 11 September several letters to editors of newspapers cited America's "aggressive" foreign policy, seen as an attempt to rule the world and unduly favor Israel, as the chief cause of radical Islamic activity.

In **Argentina**, María Hebe Pastor de Bonafini, leader of Mothers of Plaza de Mayo, said she had rejoiced when she heard about the attacks against the WTC – "It made me happy." For her, the attacks had "avenged the blood shed by so many," since "in those two towers it was decided who among us would die, lose their jobs, be massacred, be bombed." Moreover, "the fear that they instilled in us, with the persecutions, the disappearances, the torture, is now being experienced by the entire American people – the people who remained silent and applauded wars." Bonafini compared the WTC attackers to "our children" who "were also called terrorists, but were revolutionaries," and "gave their lives for a better world."

In **Venezuela** letters to mainstream papers claimed that the US attitude toward Israel was the principal cause of the radicalization of Islam, which had led to such catastrophic results. Biased American policy they maintained, had led to deep-seated Arab hatred of the United States. Venezuelan criticism of the American campaign in Afghanistan was voiced not only in the press, but also by government figures and intellectuals. In an article in the mainstream *El-Nacional*, Prof. Vera Chela from the University of Caracas expressed empathy with the terrorists' motives. It was America, she wrote, that had sown the seeds of hatred. Not only had it conducted an imperialistic policy but it had also supported the Jewish occupation of Palestine and the expulsion of its true habitants.

In **Brazil** there were conflicting viewpoints regarding the attacks, the fight against terrorism and US relations with Israel and the Jews. On the one hand, Brazilian television broadcast scenes of Palestinians rejoicing on the day of the bombing and during its aftermath, and interviewed a Palestinian living in Brazil who said she was happy to see the devastation. The revulsion to this attitude opened a crack in the usually solid support of the Palestinians. On the other hand, there were signs of increasing anti-Americanism in Brazil. For example, accusations were leveled at the United States by leading public figures, such as Judge Fabio Konder Comparato, who claimed that the United States was "a criminal nation which flouts international law and morality in its relations with other peoples, while in the name of sovereignty its policies border on international crime." Milton Temer, of the leftist Partido do Trabalho (PT), said the United States was reaping the fruits of a policy of aggressive imperialism.

Brazilian youth expressed open hostility to America on various occasions. At a street protest in September demanding better educational conditions, high school students carried posters of bin Ladin saying,

"He's innocent." In the Sao Paolo youth paper *Folhateen* a letter to the editor claimed, "I do not accept the attempt to turn bin Ladin into the devil, which CNN is doing. He is a man fighting for the freedom of his people." A survey in this paper showed that 52 percent of readers thought President Bush more of a terrorist than bin Ladin.

The special relationship between the United States and Israel was the subject of some extremely harsh commentary in the media by public figures and members of parliament. Former Administration Minister Luis Carlos Bresser Pereira blamed the United States for its position of unreserved support of Israel, which he considered had laid the ground for Islamic hatred of the United States.

Some letters to the editor in mainstream newspapers of São Paolo and Rio de Janeiro expressed extremely anti-Zionist opinions, even calling for the annihilation of the State of Israel. The well-known Brazilian intellectual Jose Arthur Giannotti viewed the new alliance against terrorism as an opportunity for a rational solution to the problem of the Middle East. "Let us agree that the history of the Middle East would be entirely different without the State of Israel, which opened a wound between Islam and the West. Can you get rid of Muslim terrorism without getting rid of this wound which is the source of the frustration of potential terrorists?"

Emir Sader, professor of sociology at the University of São Paolo and the University of Rio de Janeiro, inveighed against Jewish influence in Brazil and throughout the world. In *Folha de Sao Paulo* he wrote: "One of the reasons for the failure of US policy is the pressure of the Jewish lobby." According to Sader, "Zionism is racism, since the Arabs are second-class citizens there." Further, he claimed, "there is also a hateful Zionist lobby in Brazil, which daily brings to bear all the forces of the media in order to mold public opinion to suit the Jews, while silencing all who disagree with them."

Western Europe

Criticism of US support for Israel and empathy with Islamist terror appeared in publications of the West European extreme right, which for years had demonized Arabs/Muslims in Europe. Radical neo-Nazis joined left-wingers and Islamists in anti-American demonstrations, which were often accompanied by direct or indirect verbal attacks against Israel or the Jews.

In **Spain**, for example, the Movimiento Social Republicano (MSR) participated in demonstrations organized by Islamists and non-governmental organizations in favor of the Palestinians and in protest against the US anti-terror initiative. It should be noted that on other occasions the same group joined the xenophobic protests of residents against the opening of a Moroccan consulate in Almeria and marched in demonstrations alongside racist groups such as Blood & Honour.

In **Germany** the extreme right attempted to make political capital out of the attacks on America and the war in Afghanistan. Chanting anti-imperialist slogans with a leftist ring, Germany's National Democratic Party (NPD) and other ultra-right-wing groups demonstrated their "solidarity with the Afghan people" as well as a surprising solidarity with Muslims living in Germany. Accusing the US of waging a "war of retribution against the Islamic world," they declared "that the participation of the German government is thereby also an open declaration of war against the two million Muslims who live here."

However, extreme rightist support for the Islamist terror attacks on the US was not unanimous. The German Republikaner, for example, distanced themselves from such solidarity, and backed the American air strikes in Afghanistan. Chairman of the Republikaner Rolf Schlierer understood that "effectively fighting Islamic fundamentalist terror is in Germany's interest," since the Taliban were endangering Germany's domestic peace "by producing refugee waves and heroin."

Exploiting public fear of a terror attack, the Republikaner demanded, in the name of internal security and protection of citizens, stronger surveillance measures, especially of foreigners, asylum seekers and others who might threaten their freedom. They tried to persuade the insecure population that multiculturalism was a dangerous dream.

Some extreme right activists admitted they found it difficult to resolve the conflict between their struggle against Muslim immigration to Europe, on the one hand, and their sympathy for the fight against the US, on the other. In October 2001 NPD vice-chairman Jürgen Schön declared that "we nationalists are fighting against the economic, cultural and militaristic aspirations of the US for world domination (*Weltherrschaft*) and at the same time against the islamization of Europe, since Islamic fundamentalism represents a threat to the struggle for existence of the German people."

In France and the UK, the countries with the largest Arab/Muslim and Jewish populations, violent attacks against Jewish targets increased considerably after 11 September. In the UK, antisemitic incidents rose by 150 percent in September and October over August 2001. The figures for September and October were the second and the third highest monthly totals ever recorded. In France 44 percent of major violent incidents and attacks for the year 2001 took place in September and October.

The US

The satisfaction expressed by some extreme right groups in Western Europe following the attacks in the US created a sharp dispute with their American white supremacists allies. When the Spanish neo-Nazi *Nuevorden*, which was linked to the server of the white supremacist Stormfront, operating out of Florida, applauded the anti-American attacks, they were removed from the server with the following announcement: "We have watched with deep anger and disgust the unfeigned joy with which many 'patriots from Spain and from other countries have welcomed the attack against our own country, which has so far given you the opportunity to put information online via this site. Thousands of my fellow countrymen have been killed by the Arabs, who have also invaded your country and threaten the entire West. However, we see that many national socialists like you do whatever is possible to justify what is unjustifiable."

Organizations on the extreme right in the US – primarily hate groups and anti-government groups – reacted aggressively to the September 11 attacks and their aftermath. Some blamed American society, suggesting that toleration of homosexuals, abortions and separation of church and state had led God to punish the United States. Groups and individuals such as the neo-Nazi National Alliance, the World Church of the Creator and former Ku Klux Klan leader David Duke, one of the main activists of the American extreme right, attempted to seize what they sensed was an opportunity to channel the raw emotions felt by many Americans after the events toward targets of their own desire, mainly Jews and immigrants. On the other end of the political spectrum, some on the left blamed American oil interests or large corporations for the war in Afghanistan.

Like Islamists and commentators in the Arab world, American ultra-rightists tried to exploit the claim made in mainstream papers immediately after 11 September that the terrorists were motivated mainly by frustration and fury over American support for Israel – an assumption rejected by terrorism experts. An ADL survey released in November found that the American people overwhelmingly rejected the notion that the close US-Israeli relationship was to blame for the September 11 attacks. The survey revealed that 63 percent of Americans believed that Usama bin Ladin attacked America because "the terrorists don't like our values or way of life, not because of our relationship with

Israel." Only 22 percent thought the attack would not have occurred had the US not been such a close ally of Israel.

To hardcore antisemites, Jews were responsible for everything bad in America, up to and including the terrorist attacks. Most common among hate groups was the argument that the September 11 attacks occurred because the United States, dominated by the "Jewish lobby," supported Israel. Many extreme right groups preferred such arguments because they were more persuasive than Mossad conspiracy theories (see below). "Ever since the beginning of the last century," Arkansas-based Klan leader Thomas Robb told his followers in a November issue of his newsletter *The Torch*, "we have allowed anti-Christian Jews entrance into our Christian government under the guise of tolerance." Jews came to dominate the entertainment industry, he wrote, and "eventually captured our political parties and churches." Consequently, the US had abandoned the "Christian principles of our forefathers" and adopted a campaign of "political Zionism." As a result of the domination of the US by Jews, "we are under not a blessing but a curse for our wickedness." The New York-based newsletter *White Voice* agreed, asserting that the "Jewish State of Israel, and its Jewish supporters in the United States, in particular, the Jewish lobby which controls our Congress... have succeeded in bringing their cursed war, and their wretched enemies to America's shores." Alex Linder, editor of the Missouri-based *Vanguard News Network*, was more succinct, writing in early November that "Jews cause problems. Period."

The actions of Matt Hale of the racist and antisemitic WCOTC illustrate the energy with which white supremacists have attempted to co-opt the September 11 attacks for their own ends. After the attacks, Hale issued a press release with the headline, "Pro-Israel Policy Costs Thousands of Lives Today." The release demanded an end to US aid to Israel and the "liberation" of the US from "the manipulations of the Jews that have had such terrible consequences," Hale called for a "fervent and immediate response" in spreading this message." Within a week of the attacks, WCOTC members had distributed fliers in Phoenix, Arizona, featuring the slogan, "Let's stop being human shields for Israel," and urging Americans to "find a nationalistic government that will look after their interests and not the interests of the Jews." Members in Spokane, Washington, distributed similar fliers.

Hale himself led demonstrations in East Peoria, Illinois, in which he and his followers displayed signs with messages such as "America before Israel" and "Arabs & Jews Get Out." When the United States began its military attack in Afghanistan, Hale altered his message to suggest that the war was for the benefit of the Jews and criticized the people "chomping at the bit to annihilate the anti-JOG [Jewish Occupied Government] forces in Afghanistan." In a late October press release, Hale asserted that "this Jewish-dominated government… is quite willing to force non-Jewish Americans to become human shields." He claimed that "with each passing day, more and more white people agree with our message."

Neo-Nazi David Duke was equally opportunistic. The former Klan leader issued a statement on his website shortly after the attacks, labeling them a "day of tragedy for the wounded heart of America." Duke accused the "powerful, Zionist lobby" which dominated the media and government and whose actions caused suffering among "our people, the normal moms and pops, and sons and daughters of America." He claimed that the US was now "reaping the whirlwind," while "our masters already plan their war against the terrorism that they themselves inspired." He urged the US to "break the grip of this Zionist power in our midst."

In subsequent pronouncements, Duke elaborated on this theme, blaming the terrorist attacks on the "criminal behavior" of Israel. His organization produced a flier that claimed, "Israeli genocide against the Palestinians is paid for with our money and now our blood." Duke, too, incorporated US military actions in Afghanistan into his propaganda. "Jewish supremacist elements in the government and mass media," he said in the October 2001 issue of his *David Duke Report*, were trying to expand the actions in Afghanistan into a "massive, global war."

The National Alliance, America's largest neo-Nazi group, led by William Pierce (whose novel, *The Turner Diaries*, inspired terrorists in the 1980s and 1990s), was slower than Hale and Duke in responding to the attacks. Pierce eventually took the lead with short-wave radio broadcasts dominated by accusations against Jews. The terrorist acts, he claimed, were "a direct consequence of the American people permitting the Jews to control their government and to use American strength to advance the Jews' interest at the expense of everyone else's interests." Many more people, he warned, will be killed because of US government actions "at the behest of the Jews." Although Pierce condemned the terrorists in a later broadcast for killing so many white people in the attacks on the WTC, his message focused almost completely on Jews. "We were attacked," he said later in September, "because we have been letting ourselves be used to do all of Israel's dirty work in the Middle East." President Bush himself, Pierce said, was controlled by Jews working behind the scenes who judged "every policy by the single criterion, 'Is it good for the Jews?'"

The National Alliance propaganda machine produced fliers for members to distribute. In Pennsylvania, they contained an image of Tower Two as it collapsed with the accompanying caption, "Is Our Involvement in the Security of the Jewish State Worth This?" In Washington, DC, National Alliance members organized a demonstration outside the Israeli embassy in early November to "express the opposition of American patriots to the policies of the US government that expose Americans to terrorist attacks." Claiming to speak "on behalf of all humanity," the National Alliance expressed its concern for world peace and asserted: "The interests of the Jews does NOT [sic] outweigh the needs of the people of the world! The freedom-loving people of the world are adamant that the Jewish state immediately cease its barbaric treatment of the people whose lands it occupies illegally! Israel's continued genocidal actions leave us no alternative but to call for a total end to all American economic and military aid to Israel! Failure to address these reasonable demands will be a tacit admission to the world that Israel is a terrorist state and that Jewish interests are bent on world domination and genocide against Palestinians, Muslims and people of European ancestry!"

Thus, opportunistic antisemites such as Matt Hale, David Duke and William Pierce aimed at creating a new wave of antisemitism by convincing Americans that the terrorist attacks were the direct result of US support for Israel, and that this support stemmed from complete Jewish domination of the government. This line of argumentation was also raised by leaders of extreme black groups in the US. Malik Zulu Shabazz, national chairman of the New Black Panther Party (NBPP), claimed, for example, at a televised conference in November 2001 that "Zionism is racism, Zionism is terrorism, Zionism is colonialism, Zionism is imperialism, and support for Zionism is the root of why so many were killed on 11 September."

Central and Eastern Europe

As in Western Europe, the extreme right attempted to find a synthesis between criticism of the US, particularly its support for Israel, and its fundamental fear of Islamic infiltration into Europe. For almost a decade now antisemites of the former communist states in Eastern Europe have presented themselves, on the one hand, as true supporters of "Christian and Western values" against the machinations of world Jewry, and on the other, as allies of anti-Western, Arab and Muslim-led elements against Israel and Zionism. Thus, racist and xenophobic elements which, in principle, reject the presence in their land of non-Europeans and Muslims, make common cause with them when antisemitic and anti-Israel factors link them. This stand, adopted by the extreme right in the wake of the anti- Israel campaign in Durban, continued after 11 September.

Extremists in Eastern and Central Europe took some time to adjust their reactions to popular sentiment. The initial response of the Hungarian Justice and Life Party (MIEP) of Istvan Csurka, published in *Magyar Forum* after the attacks, was that the US had got its just desserts for its policies of world domination. MIEP, the only Hungarian party to oppose Hungarian support for the US war against terror, found its position was generally condemned.

By 20 September, it had amended its stand. In a statement published in *Magyar Forum*, the party shared its grief with the victims, but recalled other victims in the world, "those who have died of hunger, or were killed or bombed." It called for remembering "all victims of genocide" – the reference being to victims of communism. The statement concluded that the events of 11 September were not unconnected to other world events. In the same issue Csurka created a link between Durban and 11 September. He argued that the strong condemnation of Israel's racist and genocidical policies in Durban amounted to a "political Stalingrad" for Israel, the US and the forces of globalization, which they had wanted to avoid. Csurka wrote that "it is impossible to silence what is happening in Palestine, where innocent people are being killed daily – children, Palestinians who are the ancient inhabitants of the land." As for the suicide bombers who killed Israelis, Csurka implied that such deeds demonstrated the desperation of the oppressed. Against such personal actions of desperate people, the "global powers" could not launch actions of collective punishment. But, after 11 September, Csurka maintained, this had become possible: "They began with the Afghanis, but it will not end with them; that is why Arafat donated blood [to the Afghanis under US attack]."

The more sophisticated line of Romania's Greater Romania Party (GRP) continued its anti-Israel rhetoric, but was much swifter in condemning the attacks. GRP leader Corneliu Vadim Tudor, traditionally pro-Arab and especially pro-Iraq, directly linked the war against terror to his own vendetta against President Ion Iliescu, and published allegedly secret evidence that Iliescu had helped train "Hamas terrorists" in Romania in the early nineties. Unexpectedly, however, the party lowered its anti-Israel tone, while maintaining it campaign against former Jewish communists, Jewish influence in present day Romania and the destructive role played by Jewish-Israeli business interests.

THE SECOND APPROACH: "THE BIG LIE"
The theory that accusations against Muslims were merely a blind to the real identification of the perpetrators originated in the **Arab media**. Since the operation was so "successful," and required such meticulous preparatory work, Arab commentators considered it too complex and too demanding to have been carried out by an Arab/Muslim group. Seeking perpetrators who would relieve them of any blame, they resorted to conspiracy theories and suggested the attacks were "made in the USA." They accused either the Bush administration, the FBI, American extreme right organizations or oil companies of planning the attacks with the aim of furthering their own interests.

The search for likely perpetrators and conspirators "naturally" led to the Jewish connection and gave rise to a host of arguments linking Jews, Zionism and the Israeli Mossad to the attacks. They were presented as "the act of the great Jewish Zionist mastermind that controls the world's economy, media and politics." The goal of the operations was to coerce the US and NATO "to submit even more to Jewish Zionist ideology" by cultivating fears of "Islamic terrorism" and instigating a war against Islam. Only the Jews were capable of planning such an event, because it required great expertise, of which neither Usama bin Ladin nor any other Islamic organization or intelligence apparatus was capable, explained the Egyptian Shaykh Muhammad Jami`a, in the US. The attacks were straight out of *The Protocols of the Elders of Zion*, which exhorted the Jews to destroy the world in order to control it, wrote an **Egyptian** commentator, whereas a **Palestinian** observer explained that they were the result of Jewish ire and disappointment over the defeat of Al Gore and "his Zionist-American colleague" in the US presidential elections.

Posing the question as to who would have been the chief beneficiary of the attacks, it was argued that Israel stood to gain the most from the bloody operation if Arabs and Muslims were accused of perpetrating it. "The Israeli regime knows that only by inflicting such a wound and blaming it on Islamic terrorism could it wipe out any dissent to current American policy," wrote the **Iranian** daily *Jomhuri-ye Eslami*. Only a highly efficient intelligence agency with access to facilities and information inside the American system, such as the Mossad, could have been behind such attacks, the argument continued. Five Israeli youths, detained in the US for photographing the collapse of the towers, provided further "proof," in some Arab eyes, of Israeli intelligence involvement. Moreover, a **Saudi** writer even blamed the Jews for infiltrating pan-Arab and Islamic organizations that had "acted in good faith."

The most popular claim, allegedly proving the Jews' prior knowledge of the planned attacks, was the supposed absence of some 4,000 Israelis (or Jews in another version of the tale) from work in the WTC on the day of the attacks. This rumor may be traced to an accidental or deliberate misreading of an estimate by an Israeli official as to the number of Israelis living in the New York City area. It was propagated both by extreme rightist (see below) and by Islamists. "A suitable way was found to warn the 4,000 Jews who work every day at the Twin Towers to be absent from their work on 11 September 2001, and this is really what happened! Were 4,000 Jewish clerks absent by chance, or was there another reason?," asked Ra'id Salah, leader of the **Islamic movement in Israel** in its newspaper *Sawt al-Haqq wal-Hurriyya*.

This libel against Israel and American Jews appeared in publications of **American** white supremacists. Sometimes articles by Muslim writers were used by white supremacists, while articles of the latter were reprinted in the Muslim media. *The Yemen Observer*, for example, posted an article by American extreme right activist David Duke. The NY-based English-language newspaper *Muslims* reprinted an antisemitic piece by neo-Nazi William Pierce. Antisemitic articles written by Americans were reprinted also by Muslims of the Americas (MOA), a.k.a. al-Fuqra, by the Arab Students United, in *The Syria Times* and on Hizballah sites.

The extreme right in the **US** emphasized the two main arguments outlined in the Muslim press above. The Christian Identity newsletter *Scriptures for America* put it succinctly: "The Israeli Jews have much to benefit if America fights the Muslim world. And thus many suspect the behind-the-scenes action of the Mosad [*sic*]." A Texas-based newsletter *The Eagle* disclaimed "paranoia about Israeli plots," but noted that the Mossad "has the operatives with language skills who can and have infiltrated...various Islamic networks." Did the Mossad plan it? "That's hard to say," said *The Eagle*, "it's more likely Mossad encouraged and abetted or just sat back and let it happen."

Some antisemites postulated that Israel might have had partners, such as the CIA. This was the theory of Paul Hall, publisher of the antisemitic and anti-government newspaper *Jubilee*. Hall suggested that the Mossad and the CIA were the "real perpetrators," and cited *The Protocols of the Elders of Zion* to explain how Jews "will use world war to fight their enemies and achieve their goal of world government if they can't do it themselves."

Among American white supremacists, many proponents of the Jewish conspiracy theory claimed as fact the rumor that 4,000 Israelis employed at the WTC did not report for work on 11 September. This suggested to them an obvious conspiracy in which the Israeli government somehow prevented its citizens from going to the towers that day, knowing they would be attacked. Ironically, even after this hoax was completely debunked, conspiracy theorists were able to incorporate it in their propaganda. Thus Michael Collins Piper, a writer for the antisemitic *American Free Press*, claimed that the rumor was actually a straw man designed to hide Mossad foreknowledge of or involvement in the attack. "There is, however," he wrote, "good reason to believe that at least some Israelis working at the WTC may have had advance warning." Similarly, Florida antisemite Hans Schmidt, publisher of the *GANPAC Brief* newsletter, discounted the rumors of the 4,000 Israelis, but wrote that "there is no question, however, that Jews are predominant in the financial services," and that there were "relatively few Jewish names" among the initial victim lists.

Another conspiracy theory suggested that "greedy Jews" destroyed the building for the insurance money. "We've been royally conned," wrote antisemite John Bryant on his website, "by a Hebrew mish-mash of vengeful Arabs who carouse the night before their voluntary demise, Arabs who can't fly jets in any case, 'evidence' thrown around like confetti, old but newly-owned heavily-insured buildings which inexplicably fall down too soon, and jets which suddenly become uncontrollable."

Some antisemites simply combined various theories. "Did you know," stated an article on the website of the *Free American* magazine, "that in July, the Twin Towers were leased to the Silverstein Companies for a mere 668 million dollars? Did you know they were insured? Did you know that a Pakistani television station reported that none of the 4,000 Israelis and Jews who worked in the building were killed?... Could the Mossad be involved? Could this be an exaggerated case of Jewish lightning [*sic*]?"

In **Europe**, as well, Islamists, right-wing extremists and Holocaust deniers repeated the claim that Jews were behind the attacks in New York and Washington. On 21 September, for example, the imam of Valencia, **Spain**, asserted in a mosque filled with worshipers: "All the evidence shows that the Jews are guilty."

In **Romania**, the most widely circulated publication of the extreme right, *Romania Mare*, asserted that "some 4,000 Israelis and Jews were alerted not to go to their workplaces at the WTC a day before 11

September." The paper attributed the item to "news stories from various sources," but made no comment on the allegation. However, it was written in such a way that left no doubt as to its veracity.

The alleged Jewish plot behind the attacks fitted the Jewish world conspiracy theories held by some Holocaust deniers in Europe and the United States. At a gathering of Holocaust deniers in Trieste one month after the attack, the American denier Russ Granata told his audience that "the main reason why my country was attacked on 11 September was because of the US support of Israel" and "there certainly has been a lot of perceptions regarding September 11 [*sic*]. It has been reported that there was some inside trading in insurance and airline stock market shares that points to a previous knowledge of the forthcoming attack – and it has also been reported that there were some advance warnings in the Jewish-owned investment banking system." The German Holocaust denier Germar Rudolf used a similar line of argumentation, implying that the Mossad was the body that would profit most from the murder of thousands of innocent people.

Another promoter of the Jewish world conspiracy myth, Lyndon LaRouche, "the Prophet" of the LaRouche international cult, fantasized about the involvement of the Israeli army (IDF), explaining that "it is the IDF, which, as part of its war aims, has carried out an aggressive espionage and covert operations penetration of the USA."

The idea that Israel was behind the attacks and that only it could have benefited from them, served too as a propaganda theme of radical groups in **Russia** and **Ukraine**, as well as in areas with large concentrations of Muslims – Moscow, **Tatarstan**, **Bashkortostan** and **north Caucasia**. Islamic organizations, including those identified with the most radical movements in the Arab world, have increased their operations in recent years in Russia, Ukraine, the Crimean peninsula and Central Asia. They include the Muslim Brotherhood, active among Muslims in Russia, Caucasia and the Central Asian states; Hamas, active in Russia and Central Asia; Hizb-ut Tahrir al-Islami in Russia, Ukraine, Belarus, north Caucasia and Central Asia; and the Islamic Movement for the Liberation of Uzbekistan. These groups, whose growth parallels the general awakening of extremist movements in the Islamic world, and which has taken place against the background of the Russia-Chechenya conflict, is of great concern to the authorities in the former Soviet Union, which have been trying to contain and repress them in order to avoid conflict between the Slavic and Muslim populations.

ATTACKS AGAINST OTHER ETHNIC MINORITIES IN THE WAKE OF 11 SEPTEMBER

In parallel to the wave of antisemitic and anti-Israel reactions, the September 11 events triggered a series of racist attacks on Arabs and other ethnic minorities, particularly in the US. Since the acts were committed by Islamist terrorists, Arabs and Muslims became prime targets of abuse for a variety of extremists and hate groups. The hundreds of hate crimes and incidents directed against people perceived to be Arab or Muslim indicated that extremists saw the terrorist attacks as a real opportunity to exploit the deep public anger they had generated. Some hate groups specifically targeted Arabs and Muslims, while others turned their resentment of Arabs and Muslims against all immigrants.

In Mississippi, in mid-October, for example, members of the racist Nationalist Party held an "Aliens Out" protest, calling for racial profiling and the deportation of "aliens" and "suspicious characters." According to one participant, "People know that criminals, subversives and aliens must be profiled. Their looks, language and traits all need to be examined and watched, so that their threat to our American way of life can be countered and defeated." Another group, the American Nationalist Union, urged the sealing of borders with Mexico and Canada, the implementation of a ten-year moratorium on all immigration, the deportation of all illegal aliens, and the deportation of all visa and permit holders "who arouse the slightest bit of suspicion." Holocaust denier Michael Hoffman urged President Bush to "defend America from foreign invasion, by ending illegal immigration and placing a moratorium on legal immigration."

One of the organizations most active in espousing extreme anti-immigrant rhetoric was the Council of Conservative Citizens (CofCC), a large group descended from the White Citizens Councils of the segregation-era South. Within weeks of the September 11 attacks, the group displayed on its website the headline "Dirty Rotten Arabs and Muslims." An accompanying article claimed that America was now "drinking the bitter dregs of multiculturalism and diversity." Moreover, the threat of "Muslim-Arab mischief" was not confined to Usama bin Ladin, since "Arab treachery and deviousness have been a scourge since biblical times." Islam, the website asserted, "is a religion of hatred and vindictiveness!"

In the CofCC website's "Confederate Dreadnaught" editorial section, a particularly racist essay claimed that the answer to "this problem of terrorism" is to "segregate ourselves from the Arabs, Muslims, and/or all others who will do us harm," whether they are "Arab terrorists, or Chinese scientists stealing our nuclear secrets, or blacks raining murder, rape, and theft down among us." CofCC member H. Millard suggested that when US reservists were called up to fight terrorism, illegal aliens would fill their jobs and fill "the lonely nights of the women left behind." In November, a Dreadnaught essay urged Southerners to "glorify God, aided by the ethnic segregation He instituted in the Bible."

COUNTRY AND REGIONAL ABSTRACTS

(For full country reports and updates, see
http://www.tau.ac.il/Anti-Semitism/annual-report.html)

Western Europe

AUSTRIA

Austria has a Jewish population of 10,000 out of a total population of 8 million, most of which lives in Vienna.

Organized neo-Nazis have demonstrated increased self-confidence since the Freiheitliche Parteï Österreichs (FPÖ) joined the government in 2000. They have increased membership and support and intensified their activities. For the first time since 1991 they held an illegal march following a demonstration in Vienna on 13 April 2002 protesting the Wehrmacht exhibition. A leading organizer of the march, Kameradschaft Germania, is the most successful of the recently organized *Freie Kameradschaften*.

The number of extreme right racist and antisemitic crimes committed in Austria in 2001 remained virtually unchanged: the Ministry of Interior reported 337 such crimes for 2001 compared to 336 in 2000. While there were no violent antisemitic attacks, there was a great deal of anti-Jewish propaganda. Carinthian State Governor Jörg Haider, for instance, used antisemitic slurs to attack the chairman of the Jewish community (IKG), Ariel Muzicant, on several occasions.

Some antisemitic propaganda was blended with anti-American, anti-Zionist and anti-Israel expressions after the September 11 events, when the traditional support of the Austrian right for Arab nationalists was extended to sympathy for Islamic extremists. Otto Scinzi, *Aula* editor and former FPÖ parliamentary representative, described the perpetrators as "political or religious but certainly not criminal fundamentalists in the cheap sense of the word." Wiener Nachrichten Online (WNO) referred to organizations such as Hamas, Jihad and Hizballah as "liberation organizations," while Israel was accused of state terrorism and systematic genocide.

The anti-Israel rhetoric of extreme left groups sometimes borders on antisemitism. The leftist Internet site *Indymedia*, for example, published a list of "US Israelis who worked in the US under Clinton."

In 2001, police received a total of 269 complaints of alleged violations of the National Socialism prohibition law, compared to 239 in 2000. Several right-wing militants, including Hans Gamlich, Günther Reinthaler and Walter Ochensberger, were given prison terms or suspended terms in 2001/2 under this law.

Some 35,000 Jewish citizens live in Belgium out of a total population of 10 million. The two main centers of Belgian Jewry are Antwerp and Brussels. The Comité de Coordination des Organizations Juives de Belgique in Brussels is the community's umbrella organization.

Since 2000 the number of violent anti-Jewish acts reported to anti-racist and Jewish community organizations in Belgium has risen considerably. According to the Centre pour l'égalité des chances et la lutte contre le racisme (CECLR), 17 violent antisemitic acts were committed in 2001 and over 25 from January to May 2002. They included physical assaults on Jewish individuals and attacks (Molotov cocktails, stone-throwing) on synagogues. Some of the attackers were identified as youth of North African origin.

Fundamentalist Islamist circles in Belgium appear to have some influence among Muslim youth in the country, some of whom chanted antisemitic slogans during anti-Israel demonstrations organized in Brussels and Antwerp. Activists within the Maghreb community circulated anti-Jewish propaganda, despite calls for calm issued by various Islamic religious and cultural bodies. Antisemitism appears to be promoted by Islamic fundamentalist groups such as Centre Islamique de Belgique. The CECLR has lodged complaints against this group, as well as against the Arab European League, for allegedly breaching the laws against racism and revisionism.

There appears to be a correlation between the increase in antisemitic incidents and the anti-Israel atmosphere prevailing in Belgium. Since autumn 2000 antisemitic expressions in Belgium have become part of a trend to merge the terms Jews, Israelis and Zionists into a single evil entity. While criticism of Israel by many leftists in Belgium does not necessarily stem from an antisemitic worldview, antisemitic expressions can be found in anti-Israel articles by leftists, even in mainstream publications. Texts that are either blatantly antisemitic or have a more specific anti-Jewish slant circulate in political and religious circles. Several mainstream Belgian newspapers, such as Le Soir, published opinions equating the Palestinian territories with the Warsaw Ghetto, or Zionism with Nazism.

Among extra-parliamentary groups of the Belgian far right, antisemitism is less of a taboo than among their parliamentary brethren the Front national and the Vlaams Blok (VB). Although the political strategy of extra-parliamentary groups is more radical than that of these parties, the former maintain regular contact with the parliamentary representatives of right-wing extremism. In French-speaking circles, the Nation movement represents this radical far right. In the Flemish community, various far right groups associated with the VB were or remain close to antisemitic and revisionist theses.

Among extreme right groups in Belgium, as in other European countries, anti-Zionist slogans camouflage antisemitic concepts. The terms "Zionist" or "international Zionism" imply the "Jewish lobby," for example. All far right organizations demonstrate their support for the Palestinian cause in one way or another. Among Flemish nationalists, support is mainly through identification with a landless people. Among the francophones, Nation has long been the movement most closely involved in categorical support for the Palestinians.

The far right parties took advantage of the anti-Muslim atmosphere after 11 September to launch a campaign against the Arab/Muslim communities, which included violent attacks. The 2001 annual report of CECLR warns that far right organizations have taken advantage of the wave of antisemitism to aggravate tensions between these communities and Jews in the country.

Antisemitism and anti-Judaism are still very much present within fundamentalist Christian organizations and religious groups, with Jews representing one of the main targets of their politico-religious discourse. In Belgium, the Fraternité sacerdotale Saint-Pie X (FSSP X) is the chief embodiment of Christian Judeophobic fundamentalism. Most FSS-X leaders are associated with or are members of far right groups.

Despite its disbandment by Belgium's legal authorities in February 2002, the Holocaust denying Vrij historisch onderzoek has been continuing its activities under other names.

There are 7,000 Jews in Denmark, out of a total population of 5.25 million. Most Jews are concentrated in Copenhagen, but smaller communities exist in Odense and Aarhus. The central communal organization is the Mosaiske Troessamfund.

The heightened conflict between Israel and the Palestinians continued to have negative repercussions for the Jewish community in Denmark in 2001, and several violent incidents were recorded. In August 2001, for example, the apartment of an Israeli living in Sonderborg, Jutland, was burgled and vandalized following the publication of pro-Israeli comments he made to the newspaper *Jydske Vestkysten*. An American Jewish tourist wearing a kippa was attacked by Arab youths on the same day, and sustained facial injuries.

Public criticism of Israeli policy toward the Palestinians has sometimes assumed an antisemitic character. On Christmas Sunday, 30 December 2001, the provost of Copenhagen, Anders Gadegaard, delivered a sermon in the Copenhagen Cathedral, in which he compared "the ghastly story of Herod's slaughter of innocent babes in Bethlehem" to the murder of "children, women and men... by those who hold power over Bethlehem." Gadegaard subsequently published a letter in several newspapers in which he denied wishing to promote antisemitism.

Fadi Abdul Latif, one of the leaders of the Danish branch of the fundamentalist trans-national Hizb ut-Tahrir was given a suspended jail sentence in late 2002 for propagating racist propaganda and incitement to murder Jews. This virulently anti-American, anti-Israel and antisemitic movement is suspected of links with al-Qa'ida and is widely condemned by the Danish public.

The right-wing Danish People's Party, which ran on an anti-Muslim platform in the fall 2001 general election, became the third largest party in the parliament. Artist Elin Uttrup, who ran as a candidate for the Progress Party, is a member of the Danish Society for Free Historical Research, which maintains that the Holocaust is Zionist propaganda and that the Jews were not exterminated during World War II.

The neo-Nazi Danish National Socialist Party (DNSB) ran for the first time in a county council election, in November 2001. It put up candidates, led by DNSB head Jonni Hansen, for Roskilde (south of Copenhagen) county council, but won no seats.

The French Jewish community numbers between 500,000 and 600,000 out of a total population of 60 million. The largest community is in the Paris area, followed by Marseille, Lyon, Nice and Toulouse. The three main organizations of French Jewry are the Conseil Représentatif des Institutions Juives de France (CRIF), the Consistoire Central and the Fonds Social Juif Unifié (FSJU).

The marked rise in antisemitic violence since the last quarter of 2000 continued into 2001 and 2002. An unprecedented peak of more than 400 antisemitic attacks was recorded in the period fall 2000 to spring 2002. These included numerous acts of arson and vandalism against Jewish property and institutions and several violent attacks on Jewish individuals. Two Jews were knifed, in separate incidents, by youths of North African or Middle East origin in Strasbourg in January 2001. The blind rabbi of the Cannes congregation was cursed and threatened with a knife in April and the Rouen rabbi was assaulted by a man of Moroccan origin as he was leaving the synagogue in November. Noteworthy in 2002 were violent attacks on young Jewish groups. Jewish school children traveling on buses were the targets of several such acts.

Among the many arson and other attacks on synagogues, Jewish schools and clubs and cemeteries in 2001/2, the Tifefet Israel school in Sarcelles was burnt down following two attacks in February 2001, and the Gan Pardes school in Marseille was set alight in September 2001 and slogans "Death to the Jews" and "Bin Ladin will conquer" were spray painted on the walls. Several acts of desecration were recorded at Jewish cemeteries and Holocaust memorials, including Cronenboug and Schiltigheim, near Strasbourg, and the Holocaust memorial at Reims. The wave of antisemitism appeared to be both a consequence of the undeniable growth of Muslim extremism, triggered by events in the Middle East, and a phenomenon rooted in social unrest in the suburbs, mainly among disaffected youth of Muslim (North African) origin.

At all major pro-Palestinian demonstrations in Paris, a group of about 150–200 followers of the Palestinian Hamas and Lebanese Hizballah appeared, waving posters of Hamas leader Shaykh Ahmad Yassin and shouting slogans such as "Jews to the ovens" or "Jews are the enemies of humanity."

The reaction of the authorities to all these events was relatively muted, despite calls from the main Jewish organizations to enact strong law enforcement measures against the perpetrators, mainly Muslims of

North African origin. A possible explanation for the government's soft line was that, with both a presidential and a general election in the offing, it preferred not to alienate the large Muslim electorate by enacting new legislation against antisemitism. Another possibility is that the Left, which was in power until spring 2002, simply failed to understand the scope and magnitude of the wave, which contradicted all the scholarly research and surveys proving that antisemitism had been on the decline since 1945. Jewish institutions pointed to biased coverage of the Middle East conflict in the French media as a source of antisemitism, and some leading intellectuals close to the community (Alain Finkielkraut; Pierre-André Taguieff, among others) claimed that the Left was now the main bearer of anti-Israel/anti-Zionist prejudice.

Extreme right candidate National Front (NF) chairman Jean-Marie Le Pen came a surprising second in the April 2002 presidential elections, although defeated in the second round by incumbent President Jacques Chirac. After 11 September, both FN and the other far right party, the Mouvement National Républicain, toned down their antisemitic rhetoric and adopted a pro-Israel stance.

On 18 September 2002 an appeals court granted the release of Maurice Papon, 92, on the grounds of his ill-health. Papon, former general secretary of police in Gironde, 1942–44, was sentenced to ten years in prison in 1998 for deporting Jews during the German occupation. The decision angered Jewish organizations and survivor families at home and abroad and the French justice minister has appealed against the release to the Cour de Cassation (the highest court of appeal in France).

The Jewish community has more than tripled since 1989, when mass immigration of Jews from the former Soviet Union began, and is now estimated at 100,000. The largest Jewish centers are Berlin, Frankfurt, Munich and Hamburg, but Jewish communities are active in most other large urban areas. The Zentralrat acts as the umbrella organization of German Jewry. In recent years it has moved its headquarters to Berlin.

As in 2000, antisemitic manifestations carried out by radical Islamists in Germany inspired militant right-wing antisemites. The number of antisemitically-motivated crimes recorded for the year 2001 was 1,424, including 18 violent acts by the extreme right. Jewish cemeteries were once again the main targets of right-wing extremists throughout Germany, with two to three cemeteries desecrated per week, including those at Manheim, Eberswalde, Perleberg, Menterhausen, Osthessen, Dresden and Berlin. However, in 2001, synagogue desecration and the threat of arson against synagogues also became a serious concern of the Jewish communities. Such incidents included an arson attack on a synagogue in Potsdam and desecrations of synagogues in Regensburg, Dresden and Celle, where Nazi posters were found on the walls. There was a drastic increase in daubing of antisemitic slogans and symbols on houses and street walls.

After the September 11 events most of the German extreme right adopted the anti-American catchphrases of the left. Anti-American, anti-NATO and pro-Islamist articles that supported the attacks either directly or indirectly were disseminated on most Internet sites associated with both the extreme right and the ideological left. Participants at demonstrations chanted slogans such as "The USA, international center of murder," and bore banners that were pro-Palestinian and crudely anti-Israel or openly antisemitic. The calls "Solidarity with Palestine" and "Jews, Die" were found on a memorial for victims of the Ahlem concentration camp on 9 April 2002.

Although membership of the extreme right Deutsche Volksunion (DVU), Nationaldemokratische Partei Deutschlands (NPD) and Republikaner declined by about 10 percent, to 33,000 (36,500 in 2000), activists from these parties intensified their activities. The Federal Office for the Defense of the Constitution (BfVS) reported 14,725 (10,054 in 2000) politically motivated offenses in the category of "right-wing crime."

Since 1995 the extra-parliamentary extreme right has organized itself into *Freie Kameradschaften* (free associations) with no centralized structure. The cells maintain contact, *inter alia*, via the Internet. In 2001 the 150 cells recorded a 25 percent increase in membership, in marked contrast to the decline in party membership.

In 2001 some 1,300 websites were being operated by right-wing extremists in Germany, an increase of 400 percent from 1999 (330 sites). At the beginning of 2002, however, this momentum was reversed. In May 2002, providers banned 400 sites from their servers, thanks to the efforts of the police, the Jewish Community of Germany and individual initiatives to combat the dissemination of neo-Nazi propaganda on the Internet.

A study, "Mideast Reporting on the Second Intifada in the German Print Media," commissioned by the AJC and undertaken by the Duisburg Institute for Linguistics and Social Research, examined news coverage of the leading German papers *Tagesspiegel, Frankfurter Rundschau, Frankfurter Allgemeinen, Süddeutschen Zeitung, Taz, Welt* and *Spiegel* during the period September 2000–August 2001. It concluded that German Middle East press coverage was often distorted and characterized by the absence of context as well as an aggressive tone toward Israel. Instances of racist antisemitism, minimizing the Holocaust, the blood libel myth and Zionist conspiracy theories were found.

Prior to the general elections of September 2002, antisemitism became an electoral issue for the first time in postwar Germany. In April 2002 Jamal Karsli was forced to leave the Green Party after accusing Israel of using "Nazi methods." After being welcomed into the ranks of the FDP (Free Democratic Party/The Liberals) by Deputy Chairman Jürgen Möllemann, he continued to make antisemitic attacks. Möllemann had to leave the FDP in December, accused of exploiting antisemitism for electoral purposes.

Greek Jews number 5,000 out of a total population of 10 million. The two largest communities are in Athens and Thessaloniki. The Central Board of Jewish Communities in Greece (Kentriko Israelitiko Symvoulio Ellados), the main communal organization, is recognized as a legal body under state law, functioning under the jurisdiction of the Ministry of Education and Religions.

After the September 11 attacks, right-wing extremist parliamentarian George Karatzaferis claimed there were no Jews among the victims of the World Trade Center attacks because they had been forewarned by the Israeli Mossad. The most serious violent antisemitic incident in Greece in 2001 was a Molotov cocktail attack outside the synagogue of the Jewish community of Larissa, in May. In addition, the Jewish cemetery of Trikala was desecrated in April for the fifth time since 1993, and graffiti and swastikas appeared in the Jewish cemetery of Xanthe (Thrace), and on the Holocaust monument in Kastoria (Macedonia).

Chrissi Avgi (Golden Dawn), the main neo-Nazi organization in Greece, held an anti-immigrant march in Athens on 16 June. The group is active within universities, high schools and football fan clubs, which it considers its main recruiting grounds. About 300 activists operate in ten major cities. They publish a weekly, *Chrissi Avgi*, as well as the magazine *Antepithessi* (Counter-Attack), which contains an English supplement.

The year 2002, particularly from the end of March, witnessed a sharp rise in antisemitic manifestations. A comprehensive report prepared by the Greek Helsinki Monitor (GHM) and the Minority Rights Group – Greece (MRG-G) lists numerous examples of antisemitic expressions in the course of an anti-Zionist and anti-Israel media campaign in Greece in this period. These included classic allegations about a world Jewish-Zionist conspiracy as well as blood libel.

In April 2002, the Central Board of Jewish Communities protested the comparison made in the press between the extermination of the Jews in the Holocaust and Palestinian losses in the conflict with Israel. In this month alone, Jewish cemeteries in Ioannina and Macedonia were desecrated and the Holocaust memorial in Thessaloniki was vandalized.

Some 30,000 Jews live in Italy out of a total population of 57 million. The largest communities are in Rome and Milan; smaller communities exist in Turin, Florence, Livorno, Trieste, Genoa and several other cities. The Unione delle Comunità Ebraiche Italiane (UCEI), the roof organization of Italian Jewry, represents the community in official matters and provides religious, cultural and educational services.

The rising trend in antisemitism observed in the year 2000 continued into 2001/2. Moreover, antisemitic manifestations increased as of autumn 2001 to a peak that continued into 2002. About one hundred antisemitic incidents were reported, including violent acts and propaganda (in printed articles and on the Internet, graffiti on city walls, e-mail sent to websites dealing with Judaism, letters sent to Jewish institutions or individuals and leaflets). Skinheads were involved in two violent assaults on Jewish individuals: a 15-year-old Jewish boy from Milan in January 2001 and a Roman Jewish lawyer in January 2002.

The impact of the Israeli-Palestinian conflict was a leading cause in the escalation of antisemitism. From the outset the most vocal organizations supporting the Palestinian side were extreme left-wing and anti-globalization groups and the Catholic camp. Later they were joined by extreme right groups, which exploited the anti-Israel/anti-Jewish atmosphere to intensify their antisemitic activity. In articles and letters to the editor in mainstream papers, and especially in the extreme left press (for example, *Il Manifesto*, *La Fucina*, *La Rivista del Manifesto* and *Spartaco*), many Italians equated Israel with Nazi Germany, and the Palestinians with the Jews of that era, and used expressions such as "genocide" and "concentration camps" to describe events in the conflict. Pro-Palestinian/anti-Israel demonstrations came to a peak on 6 April 2002 with a national rally in Rome on 6 April 2002, under the slogan "For Peace in the Middle East." This gathering, organized by the radical left and anti-globalization groups, turned out to be violently anti-Israel, with young men dressed as suicide bombers. As of April 2002 a change of tone appeared in the Italian media, reflected in articles and letters by readers expressing concern with the rise in antisemitism.

After the initial shock of the September 11 attacks, anti-Americanism was manifested not only by right- and left-wing extremists (including a minority in the right-wing Alleanza Nazionale, a coalition partner in the Berlusconi government), but also by some radical parties (the communist parties, the Greens, Movimento Sociale–Fiamma Tricolore) and intellectuals (such as the writer Aldo Busi, the historian Franco Cardini). The communist *Manifesto* (6 March 2002) repeated the conspiracy theory according to which the Mossad knew in advance about the attack on the World Trade Center and did nothing to prevent it. Moreover, it seemed that at least one-quarter of the Italian public, representing both left and right, were sympathetic to, or understanding of, bin Ladin's position.

It should be noted that the alleged "omnipotence" of the North American Jewish lobby (and of the Israeli secret service) is a theme that appears (although infrequently and with different nuances) in all Italian publications (see, for example: Ennio Caretto, "In America la lobby ebraica oscura la presenza araba" [In America the Jewish Lobby Obscures the Arab Presence], *Il Corriere della Sera*, 10 April 2002). On 28 October 2001, following the assassination of Israeli Minister Rehavam Ze'evi and the Israeli army's entry into Bethlehem and Beit Jalla, an article by the well-known progressive journalist Barbara Spinelli appeared in the Torino paper *La Stampa*. Under the title "Ebraismo senza 'mea culpa'" (Judaism without "Mea Culpa"), Spinelli claimed among other things that the time had come for Diaspora Jews to abandon their dual loyalties and break their "blood ties" to Israel. The Jewish people, she contended, put their alleged religious-historical rights ahead of the rights of other peoples and behaved as if God allowed them to live in a state of absolute freedom while the rest of humanity lived in the "harsh kingdom of necessity." The article provoked a lengthy debate on the newspaper's website, with many supporting Spinelli's arguments.

An estimated 30,000 Jews live in the Netherlands today out of some 16 million inhabitants. The majority live in Amsterdam. Dutch Jewry is represented by three councils, based on affiliation: the Nederlands Israelitisch Kerkgenootschap, the Verbond van Liberaal Religieuze Joden and the Portugees Israelitisch Kerkgenootschap.

The rise in antisemitism noted since 1997 became more acute and serious in nature with the outbreak of the second intifada in September/October 2000. Six violent antisemitic acts were recorded in 2001 and six in the first four months of 2002. In addition, there was a steep increase in threats to use violence and in abusive language against Jews, as well as in harassment of Jewish schoolchildren. In August 2001 a Jewish woman was threatened at knife point in Amsterdam and called "a filthy Jew," and in 2002 another Jewish woman was beaten after trying to prevent the burning of an Israeli flag at a pro-Palestinian demonstration. An American youth was kicked and beaten and his skullcap taken; a Jewish boy was spat upon, pursued by someone who held a swastika over his head and called "rotten Jew, dirty child murderer." There were other numerous incidents of abuse in 2001/2, especially directed at Jews on their way to or from synagogue, but many cases were not even reported. There were two serious desecrations of Jewish cemeteries in 2001, one at Oosterhout in April and the other at Zaltbommel in June. Gravestones were daubed with swastikas and inscriptions such as "Juden raus" (70 gravestones at Oosterhout and 7 at Zalbommel).

The seriousness of the incidents in the Netherlands is highlighted by the fact that an increasing number of Jews are becoming victims of antisemitic violence and abuse. Until recently, no Jew since World War II had been threatened with a pistol or had Jewish children canceled their membership in football clubs because of acts of violence directed against them, and Jews could wear skullcaps or display car stickers with a Star of David, without suffering physical or verbal abuse. Many involved in antisemitic acts have been identified as dislocated youth from the Moroccan community in Amsterdam, who share a sense of solidarity with the Palestinians, and are influenced by Arab broadcasts on the conflict as well as by antisemitic propaganda in the Arab world. However, it should be noted that most of those who gave the Hitler salute or vandalized the Jewish cemeteries in Oosterhout and

Zaltbommel were native Dutch, not second-generation Moroccan youths.

In April 2002 about 20,000 people took part in a national demonstration organized by the Palestine Committee and Committee for Moroccan Workers in the Netherlands). Participants displayed antisemitic banners, with slogans such as "Sharon is Hitler," "Hamas, Hamas, Jews to the gas" and "Death to the Jews." Individual members or branches of several Islamist groups linked to trans-national terrorist networks are being monitored by the Dutch security services. These include the Algerian Groupe salafiste pour la Prédiction et le Combat and Takfir wal Hijra; the Egyptian al-Jamaʻa al Islamiyya and Islamic Jihad; and the Turkish Kaplan (Caliphate), which was banned in Germany.

Following the September 11 events, the country experienced a brief spate of anti-Muslim violence, directed mainly against mosques and Islamic schools (vandalism, graffiti, arson attempts, as well as phone and letter threats). Several Nederlandse Volksunie and Stormfront Nederland members were arrested in connection with these incidents.

The Jewish population of Spain numbers 14,000 out of a total population of 39.1 million. The main Jewish centers are Madrid and Barcelona. Smaller communities are located in other cities and towns, notably Málaga, as well as Ceuta and Melilla in Spanish North Africa. The Federación de Comunidades Israelitas de España (Federation of Jewish Communities in Spain) represents Jewish interests to the government.

Islamic groups and individuals in the North African autonomous cities of Ceuta and Melilla manifested extreme antisemitic behavior during the year 2001, especially after the September 11 events. In Ceuta Muslim youths burned the US flag, displayed the Palestinian one and shouted anti-Jewish slogans. They also threw Molotov cocktails at a Catholic church and vandalized Jewish shops. In Melilla the Jewish cemetery was desecrated and when a delegation led by the president of the Jewish community came to inspect the damage, its members were abused with antisemitic and pro-bin Ladin taunts.

Earlier, in June 2001, Muslims in Melilla participated in a pro-Palestinian demonstration, at which they chanted antisemitic slogans and carried placards reading, "Jews, dregs of humanity," "[Jews] you are going to die" and "Hebrews, you kill four thousand people a day." Israeli flags were burned, swastikas were displayed, and the youngest demonstrators (some only aged only five or six) offered their "chests against Zionist bullets." NATO, the European Union, the UN and the US were described as "friends of the Zionist invaders and enemies of the Muslims." The Islamic association Badr allegedly declared its support for the demonstration.

Some neo-fascist groups in Spain also celebrated the September 11 attacks and joined Islamic and pro-Palestinian groups in demonstrations against the US and Israel. The neo-fascist Movimiento Social Republicano led by Juan Antonio Llopart and Juan Antonio Aguilar, for example, was actively pro-Palestinian, participating in demonstrations together with non-governmental organizations and Islamic groups. At these events, supporters bore placards saying, "Palestine will overcome" and "Against the [US] Terrorist War: Neither war nor NATO. No to intervention."

Sweden has a Jewish population of about 18,000 out of a general population of 8.9 million. The majority, approximately 10,000, live in the larger cities, Stockholm, Göteborg and Malmö. Smaller Jewish communities can be found in Boras, Uppsala, Norrköping and Helsingborg. The various communities are independent, but linked through the Council of Swedish Jewish Communities.

By hosting the January 2000 Stockholm International Forum on the Holocaust, attended by forty-five heads of state who declared that the Holocaust "challenged the foundations of civilization," Sweden became a leading force for raising awareness of the Shoah. Its Living History Project has become a model of Holocaust education. As an outcome of that meeting plans were announced to establish the European Institute of Jewish Studies in Sweden, Paideia. The institution was inaugurated in September 2001 with an academic conference. In January 2001, Stockholm was the venue for the Second International Forum for Combating Intolerance, which had as its goal "counteracting and preventing xenophobia, racism, antisemitism and other extremist ideas and movements."

Unofficial figures for 2001 showed a rise in the number of antisemitic incidents, due mainly to the escalation of the Israeli-Palestinian conflict. In two violent incidents in Stockholm, two Israeli Jews were beaten by two Palestinians in January 2001 and a Jewish youth was assaulted by a skinhead in September. In another incident in March, a rabbi and his son were harassed in Stockholm by two men who shouted antisemitic slurs. At least 16 telephone threats were received by the Göteborg Jewish community. A Göteborg rabbi was also the target of several bomb threats, forcing the police to evacuate his building. In June the wall of the old Jewish cemetery in Malmö was smeared with antisemitic graffiti. A memorial to Raoul Wallenberg was defaced with spray paint on 24 August 2001, a day after it was unveiled by King Carl Gustav XVI of Sweden in the presence of UN Secretary-General Kofi Annan and diplomats from various countries. Wallenberg helped thousands of Jews escape deportation to death camps from Nazi-occupied Hungary

A sharp increase in incidents was reported in the first months of 2002. Pro-Palestinian rallies were characterized by a strong left-wing element, whose slogans were sometimes antisemitic, as in equation of the Star of David with the swastika. Left-wing antisemitism was also noted on the Internet, such as the Indymedia site.

The September 11 events caused a split in the xenophobic extreme right, with the Sweden Democrats taking a hard-line anti-Muslim and anti-Arab stand, and Nazi organizations such as the National Socialist Front adopting an antisemitic and anti-Israel position. The *Swedish National Socialist*, homepage of the NSF, described the events as "an attack on the New World Order," which they view as a Jewish conspiracy.

Developments on the far right have left the Sverigedemokraterna (Sweden Democrats – SD) the single surviving xenophobic party, with a nation-wide organization and potential to expand its electoral base. In its campaign for the September 2002 general election, the party courted the xenophobic fringe in the hope of establishing itself as the single, undisputed "nationalist" alternative. A breakaway group, Nationaldemokraterna (National Democrats – ND), was formed by hardcore SD activists in August 2001.

Sweden remains a major producer of white power music, although a growing proportion of records, videos and other merchandise is created for markets outside Sweden (Germany being the largest). The two leading white power companies are Nordland, owned by American white supremacist William Pierce (died July 2002), and Ragnarock Records, run jointly by former Norwegian Nazi leader Erik Blücher (aka Erik Nilsen) and Blood & Honour/Scandinavia.

Some 18,000 Jews live in Switzerland out of a total population of 7.13 million. More than half live in the German-speaking part of the country. The umbrella organization of Swiss Jews is the Schweizerischer Israelitischer Gemeindebund/Fédération Suisse des Communautés Israélites (SIG/FSCI). The German-language Jewish publications *Israelitisches Wochenblatt* and *Jüdische Rundschau* merged under the name *Tachles* in April 2001.

A rise in the number of antisemitic incidents was recorded in 2001, mainly in the form of graffiti, insults, hate mail and threats. The murder of an Israeli rabbi, Abraham Grünbaum, who was visiting Zurich in June, may have been antisemitically motivated, but no one claimed responsibility and no clues were found at the scene of the crime.

Anonymous antisemitic tracts, posters and stickers were distributed in schools and mailboxes and posted in streets; they denounced a Jewish conspiracy, Jewish racism and Jewish responsibility for Switzerland's problems.

The September 11 events revealed ties between far right circles and Islamic extremists. Ahmed Huber, a Swiss Holocaust denier who converted to Islam, serves as a link between the extreme right and Islamist groups. Huber is a director of the Lugano-based company Al-Taqwa, which is suspected of financing the September 11 attacks. Al-Taqwa, which changed its name to Nada Management Organization, was raided by the police after the attacks. In November 2001, Huber organized in Lucerne a gathering "against world Zionist domination and the American Satan." He also gave a lecture to the neo-pagan Avalon circle, headed by Roger Wüthrich. Far right extremists admire Muslims and share a common enmity toward Jews and Americans

The situation in the Middle East generated a wave of reactions in Switzerland, mostly supportive of the Palestinians and some of them downright antisemitic. Many demonstrations were held to support the Palestinian cause. Slogans and leaflets at these demonstrations denounced "the massacre of the Palestinian people" and "Israel's apartheid policy," and alleged Israeli responsibility for the September 11 attacks. Letters to the editor and media commentators blurred the distinction between Jews and Israelis and compared the Sharon government to the Nazi regime.

Israel's response to the intifada was exploited by some Swiss citizens to retaliate in kind against criticism of Swiss behavior in the matter of

Holocaust victims' assets in Swiss banks. "You lectured us on morality and justice, but look at how you treat the Palestinians," was a common accusation in letters to the editors of local newspapers as well as in public forums.

The national debate over Switzerland's stand during World War II came to an end with the publication in March 2002 of the last of twelve reports of the Bergier Independent Experts' Commission. The findings showed that Switzerland's discriminatory asylum policy contributed to the Holocaust, that Swiss neutrality was manipulated to serve political and economic interests, and that banks did not actively collaborate with the Nazis during the war.

Reactions to antisemitism were scarce outside the Jewish community. Most political, social, religious and other NGO organizations distanced themselves from the Middle East conflict, or openly adopted a position in favor of the Palestinians and refused to condemn antisemitic manifestations.

Forty-four Swiss extreme right homepages had been closed by the provider Yahoo! by February 2001, as a result of pressure by Aktion Kinder des Holocaust. The organization is working to persuade other providers to block access to, or close, other Swiss far right sites.

The Jewish community of the United Kingdom numbers 280,000, out of a total population of 58 million. Two-thirds of the community is concentrated in Greater London. Other major Jewish centers are Manchester, Leeds and Glasgow. The Jewish population has experienced a marked decline since 1967, mainly due to a low birthrate, intermarriage and emigration.

The central organization of British Jewry is the Board of Deputies of British Jews (BoD). Security and defense activity is organized through the Community Security Trust (CST). The main community papers are the 160-year-old *Jewish Chronicle*, the *Jewish Telegraph* published simultaneously in northern cities, and the *London Jewish News*. Two Jewish websites are based in the UK: *totallyjewish.com* and *jewish.co.uk*, carrying national and international news.

Despite a 23 percent decline in 2001 from the previous year, there has been an upward trend in antisemitic incidents over the last four years, and a tendency toward more violent attacks on the Jewish community. A total of 310 antisemitic incidents were reported during 2001; thirty-two percent of the year's total occurred during September and October, after the September 11 attacks. There were 41 physical assaults against members of the community, including one life-threatening attack, compared with 53 assaults in 2000. Incidents of damage and desecration of property increased to 90 incidents in 2001 compared to 73 in 2000. Most antisemitism in the UK today emanates from militant Islamist and other Muslim groups. Public demonstrations by the "Stop the War Coalition," which brought together far left and Islamic militants to protest American action against Afghanistan after 11 September, were the venue for antisemitic invective by Islamic militants.

Anti-Israel argumentation has frequently overstepped the line and become outright antisemitism, a trend evidenced among the far and the liberal left. One example was the publication of an article by Faisal Bodi, former student activist and now editor of the electronic Muslim affairs journal *ummahnews.com*, in *The Guardian* in January, entitled "Israel Simply Has No Right to Exist." In February 2002 the left-liberal weekly magazine *New Statesman* was widely criticized for publishing anti-Israel and antisemitic material, including a front cover which showed a Magen David piercing the Union Jack symbol of Britain, under the headline "A Kosher Conspiracy?"

The most active proponents of Holocaust denial are now Islamist groups. In April the pro-Hamas *Palestine Times* published an article, "Could Zionism Lie about the Holocaust too," in which the writer Khalid Amayreh took up the theme, subsequently repeated in other Islamist publications, that Zionists have told so many lies about history that it is not inconceivable that they have lied about the Holocaust.

Holocaust Memorial Day in 2001 (27 January) elicited a number of negative responses from some sections of the Muslim community. The Muslim Council of Britain, an umbrella body representing Muslim organizations, stated that it would not attend the national event for the second year running, because it excluded current acts of "genocide" in Kashmir and Palestine. In February Omar Bakri Muhammed, founder of al-Muhajiroun (AM), the most active Islamist group in the UK, posted a message to the AM website in which he wrote: "How could Hitler kill 6,800,000 Jews when there was only [sic] 3,500,000 Jews living in Europe?"

The strengthening of Britain's Race Hatred laws in two separate acts of legislation in 2001 has effectively put a stop to the publication and distribution of overt antisemitic and Holocaust denial propaganda, but not of the more subtle kind, including denigration of the Holocaust and of Jewish claims to restitution. Two anti-terrorism acts were passed in 2001, one after the September 11 attacks.

Former Soviet Union and Eastern Europe

The Jewish Community

About 510,000 Jews remained in the former Soviet Union at the beginning of 2002. Some 445,000, 84.3 percent of the total, lived in Russia, Ukraine or Belarus, while 40,000 resided in the six Muslim states of the former Soviet Union, 20,000 in the three Baltic states and the rest in Moldova and Georgia.

The population has diminished by about 1.8 million people since 1989: about 930,000 emigrated to Israel, 570,000 to Western countries, and the negative birth rate accounted for about 290,000.

Although there are significant differences from country to country, in all the republics of the former Soviet Union, Jews engage in organized activity and enjoy the right to emigrate.

There are 430 Jewish organizations and religious foundations, which undertake a variety of activities, mostly supported by Israel and by Jewish organizations in the West. These include Jewish education (about 30,000 children and young people), aid to the needy, support for Jewish traditional and cultural activities and preserving the memory of the Holocaust. They publish about 35 newspapers and periodicals which are distributed among the Jewish population. However, no more than 10 percent of the entire Jewish population participates in these activities.

The trend toward increasing involvement of local authorities in Jewish communal affairs, which began in 2000 with the encouragement of the government, continued into 2001 and 2002. The political objective is evident: to minimize the influence of Israel and the West on the local Jewish population, to curtail Zionist elements in Jewish activities, to bind the Jewish communities more closely to local authorities, and finally to reduce Jewish emigration, especially to Israel.

Antisemitic Activity – General Characteristics

No country of the former Soviet Union includes antisemitism in its official policy or state ideology. Jews continue to be prominent in economic, cultural and political life, some serving in leadership positions in Jewish organizations as well. There was, however, a trend toward diminished political involvement by Jews in 2001 and 2002, particularly in Russia, because of the change in government there. In Ukraine, Belarus, the Baltic states and especially in Russia, widespread antisemitic activity, which differed according to the political configuration in each country, continued as in the recent past, but ceased to be used as a political tool, as it had been in the late 1990s in the Slavic countries in particular (for more on this theme, see http://www.tau.ac.il/Anti-Semitism/asw99-2000/mathyl.htm). Today antisemitism in those states is characteristic of extremist fringe groups, which in Russia engage in vandalism, hooliganism and propaganda on a much greater scale than in. the other countries of the former Soviet Union.

Islamic Movements

In most of the countries of the former Soviet Union the activity of extremist Islamic organizations increased between 2000 and 2002. These organizations were established and are funded by Islamic fundamentalists, mostly from Saudi Arabia and Kuwait. They promote an anti-Russian attitude, which has spread rapidly among the Muslim population (about 25 million people) in the context of the continuing hostilities in the northern Caucasus and is regarded as a Muslim-Christian struggle. They also foster an anti-Ukrainian stance, due to persecution of the Tatars in the Crimean peninsula. Economic difficulties and political repression in Central Asia, particularly in Uzbekistan, Tajikistan and Kyrgyzstan, which have long been subject to the Taliban ideology from Afghanistan, facilitate dissemination of the Islamist doctrine in these countries.

Islamist organizations include the Muslim Brotherhood (49 branches in Russia, and others in Central Asia and the Caucasus), the Muslim Committee of Asia (Russia and Central Asia), Hizb ut-Tahrir al-Islamiyya (Russia, Azerbaijan, Belarus, Ukraine, Kazakhstan, Kyrgyzstan), Hamas (Russia, Central Asia), Center for Islamic Development (Kyrgyz), Adalat (Uzbekistan) and Tovba (Azerbaijan, Kyrgyzstan, Uzbekistan). These organizations reflect the anti Israel and anti Jewish attitudes of the parent organizations in the Middle East, which finance the dissemination of their propaganda. Although it is in their vital interest to prevent these organizations from allying themselves with the Chechen rebels in northern Caucasia, the authorities find it difficult to control them. The Jewish population, which often lives in close proximity to the Muslim population, suffered no violence at their hands in 2001/2, but the threat of future violence is present.

Uzbekistan, Kyrgyzstan and Tajikistan have long been subjected to pressure from the Islamic Movement of Uzbekistan, under Juma

Nomangani, which seeks to set up a caliphate, in the Fergana Valley, a meeting point of these three Central Asian countries. Hizb al-Tahrir al-Islamiyya, which has declared its intention of establishing an Islamic state in the whole of Central Asia, the Caucasus and in heavily Muslim-populated areas of Russia, is also active. There is still a sizable Jewish population in Central Asia, mainly Bucharans.

The trial of Mubariz Aliev, commander of Jeishullah (Army of God), and twelve members of his organization, ended on 22 September 2000 in Baku. They were found guilty of a long list of murders and acts of terror, including armed robbery of the European Development Bank in Baku, in December 1998, and planning a terrorist attack on the American embassy in Uzbekistan in August 1999. In Uzbekistan a branch of the World Conference of Muslim Youth still operates, under a Saudi Arabian citizen, Muhammad Salam 'Abd al-Hamid, and a number of Somali and Yemeni citizens. This group also recruits and trains potential fighters in Chechnya, and disseminates Islamic propaganda and virulent antisemitism. Baku is still home to a large number of Jews.

About 230 Jewish organizations of various types are active in about 120 Russian cities with a sizable Jewish population (Moscow, St. Petersburg and Novosibirsk being the largest). They are gathered under several umbrella organizations: the Russian Jewish Congress (REK), the Federation of Jewish Communities in Russia (FEOR), the Federation of Jewish Communal Organizations of Russia (Va'ad), and the Euro-Asian Jewish Congress (EEK). Organized Jewish activity involves only about 10 percent of the Russian Jewish population and is not a major factor in the life of much of Russian Jewry.

In contrast to the situation in the late 1990s, political antisemitism is no longer an issue in Russia, due to the Putin administration's usurpation of far right and far left ideologies and the fact that very few identified Jews serve in the government. However, the emergence of a new and very violent generation of ultra-nationalists and of extremist Islamist organizations, as well as reports of several serious antisemitic incidents in the first half of 2002, is cause for concern.

There were 35 antisemitic incidents in 19 Russian cities in 2001, compared to 18 incidents in 13 Russian cities in 2000. They included physical attacks, among them attempts to kill – in one case successfully, in May, during an arson attack on a well-known Moscow restaurant. In another brutal incident on February a Habad representative was attacked by 15 thugs near the Marina Rocha synagogue. There were 12 attacks in eight cities (four in Moscow) on synagogues and community property, including arson or damage by stone-throwing. In the first half of 2002, 17 incidents of a clearly antisemitic nature were carried out in 12 cities, and were similar in nature to those perpetrated in 2001.

The continuing economic crises, the war in the northern Caucasus, mass migration to central Russia, especially of Muslims and Caucasians from former Soviet states, and Islamic revivalism among Russian Muslims, have resulted in a sharp increase in racism among Slavic people. New, extreme nationalist groups have sprung up throughout the country, but mainly in the large cities, some with Nazi ideologies, but with antisemitism still marginal at this time. Militant skinhead groups include the RNS (Russian National Alliance), White Power, Totenkopf, United Brigade 88, Hammerskins – Russia, and Blood & Honour.

At the beginning of 2002, the Russian Federal Security Service (FSB) announced that it had uncovered cells of the Muslim Brotherhood movement in 49 of Russia's administrative regions, as well as in other

FSU states. It stated that the leaders of the Russian Muslim Brotherhood coordinated their activities with Islamic terrorist organizations in the Middle East (al-Jama'a al-Islamiyya, al-Jihad al-Islami), as well as with Usama bin Ladin, and Islamist terror organizations in Bosnia (former Yugoslavia).

Despite Putin's strong condemnation of nationalist and religious xenophobia and extremism, the reaction of the authorities to antisemitism and racism has been irresolute. However, the Duma (parliament) has been considering toughening the laws against racism and xenophobia, possibly by enforcing a ban on extremist and racist organizations.

Some 260 Jewish organizations and religious communities are active in about 120 cities, 44 of them in Kiev. They are gathered under a large number of umbrella organizations, principally the Union of Jewish Communities, the Associated Jewish Organizations and Communities, and the Jewish Confederation. There is intense rivalry over which organization should represent the community to the local authorities, to Jewish organizations abroad and to the State of Israel.

While the number of violent antisemitic incidents in 2001 remained almost on the same level as in the previous year, there was a steep rise in the first half of 2002. There were three violent incidents in 2001, compared to four in 2000: two cemetery desecrations and a shooting at a synagogue in Harson on 25 May. Thirteen antisemitic acts were recorded in the first half of 2002, largely in the provinces. Antisemitic slogans were scrawled on walls and windows were smashed at Jewish institutions and sites in several cities. Two Jordanian students assaulted a woman wearing a Star of David chain in a Dnepropetrovsk restaurant. Skinheads, who are beginning to organize in Ukraine, as they are in Russia, were responsible for a number of the attacks, mainly in Kiev and Dnepropetrovsk.

It should be noted that, in contrast to Russia, antisemitism has played almost no role in political and economic rivalries in Ukraine in the last decade. Blaming Russia rather than the Jews for the worsening economic and social situation is evidence of a change in attitude toward the latter, who play a much more modest role in the political, public and economic life of Ukraine than they do in Russia. Ukrainian antisemitism is also moderated by Ukrainian aspirations to be accepted into NATO and a desire to shake off Russian political pressure.

Antisemitism is integral to the ideologies of both Islamist groups and a number of small ultra-nationalist groups. Ukraine's Muslim population, located mostly in the Crimean peninsula, is largely Tatar. Islamist groups among this population are connected to the international al-Jama'a al-Islamiyya. These organizations maintain a wide network of religious, educational and propaganda activities, aided by the mass communication means they own (newspapers and radio stations), and even have a military base where they train Tartars to join Chechen rebels fighting the Russian army in the northern Caucasus. It should be noted that members of the Ukrainian nationalist and antisemitic UNA UNSO also fight in

Chechnya against the Russian army, and that Islamists and ultra-nationalists have found a common cause in their hatred for Jews.

The influence of ultra-nationalist groups in Ukraine has been waning, and the circulation of their periodicals, such as *Nezborim Natzia*, published by the State Independence of Ukraine, *Neskorena Natzia*, *Idealist; Za Vilnu Ukrainu* and *Samostina Ukraina*, has also been declining rapidly. The antisemitic content of these publications has decreased, perhaps in response to an order of the Kharkhov court to the intellectual, government-funded association PROSVIT to cease publication of their antisemitic youth journal *Djereltze*, on 8 December 2000.

The 80,000 Jews living in Hungary, out of a total population of 10.55 million, constitute the largest Jewish community in Eastern Europe outside the borders of the former Soviet Union. The great majority live in Budapest, with smaller communities in large urban centers such as Miskolc and Debrecen, as well as in smaller cities. The Federation of Hungarian Jewish Communities (Mazsihisz) is the main body of Hungarian Jewry.

The racist and xenophobic Hungarian Justice and Life Party (MIEP), which had hoped to become a decisive factor in the survival of the center-right coalition government in the May 2002 general elections, did not pass the electoral threshold. During the election campaign, one of the bitterest in Hungary's post-communist history, many Hungarian Socialist Party electoral posters were defaced by slogans, such as "Israeli interests are behind the Socialists." Following the formation of the new center-left government, MIEP leader Istvan Csurka claimed in the party's weekly mouthpiece *Magyar Forum* that Hungary was ruled by the "soczionists" (*szocionista*, in Hungarian). In the wake of the UN World Conference against Racism in Durban and the September 11 attacks in the US, he asserted that "the downtrodden of the world are clearly saying that Zionism is a racist ideology, and the US is a power carrying out genocide."

Pannon Radio station identifies with the MIEP line, and "Sunday Journal," a popular Sunday radio show on Hungarian state radio, has become a major forum for airing nationalist and extremist views, as well as criticism of Jewish issues. In addition, the weekly *Magyar Demokrata* has become a regular forum for the publication of antisemitic, anti-Israel and anti-Zionist articles. Following 11 September, *Demokrata* quoted from dubious sources of alleged Israeli knowledge of, if not direct involvement in, the terrorist acts, because they would serve world Jewish and US interests.

Antisemitic manifestations were reported at soccer matches (slogans such as "The train is leaving for Auschwitz.") and at far right demonstrations. They were also evident during MIEP demonstrations in Budapest in March 2001 and 2002 commemorating the 1849–49 revolution, as well as at a demonstration of skinheads that attempted to break up a Chanuka celebration in the center of Budapest in December 2002.

The "judeo-bolshevik" theme is still frequently raised so as to portray the Jews as the source of all Hungary's misfortunes, and is evident in various publications in addition to those of the extreme right. Thus, in its issue of 23 June 2001 the periodical *Our Justice 56*, "the independent journal of the 1956 freedom fighters and the victims of communist persecutions," mentions repeatedly the Jewish origin of communist leaders such as Bela Kun and Matyas Rakosi.

A troubling trend in the past few years has been the gradual expansion of a discourse minimizing and relativizing the Holocaust. Much extremist effort is also focused on condemnation of any type of memorial activity related to the Holocaust in which Hungarian participation is recalled, and of Jewish demands for compensation from Hungary. Additionally, the incorporation of activities in the school curriculum commemorating and educating about the Holocaust is vehemently rejected by extremists.

The "House of Terror" caused great controversy when it was opened in 2001. Supported by the then center-right government, and directed by Maria Schmidt, an adviser to Prime Minister Viktor Orban , the museum documents the Arrow Cross terror of late 1944 and the Stalinist terror of the late 1940s–early 1950s, allegedly led by people whose Jewish origins are clearly evident, but it ignores the antisemitic policies and legislation of the Horthy period.

Leading figures of the Hungarian Jewish community have voiced concern over the impact of antisemitism in present-day Hungary. Several months before the 2002 general elections, Peter Tordai, president of the Federation of Hungarian Jewish Communities, spoke of "frightening antisemitic tendencies in Hungary." Tordai criticized the silence of former Prime Minister Viktor Orban and his tacit courting of the extremist MIEP. Tordai also urged the Hungarian government and lawmakers to hasten legislation on racism, Holocaust denial and specifically antisemitism.

There are some five to ten thousand Jews in Poland out of a total population of close to 40 million. Most Jews live in Warsaw, Wroclaw, Krakow and Lodz, but there are smaller communities in several other cities. There are virtually no Jews in the eastern part of Poland where once large, important communities existed, such as those of Lublin and Bialystok.

The Union of Jewish Religious Communities (Zwiazek Kongregacji Wyznania Mojzeszowego), or Kehilla, and the secular Jewish Socio-Cultural Society (Towarsztwo Spoleczno-Kulturalne Zydowskie), or Ferband, are the two leading communal organizations and these, together with other Jewish groups, are linked by membership in the KKOZRP, which acts as an umbrella organization. The leading Jewish publications are the monthly *Midrasz*, *Dos Jidische Wort*, *Jidele* for youth and *Sztendlach* for primary school children. Significantly, all of these publications appear in Polish, except for *Dos Jidische Wort*, which is published in a bi-lingual Yiddish-Polish edition.

In April 2001, President Kwasniewski vetoed legislation that would have provided for the restoration of private property to Polish citizens only – clearly discriminating against Jewish claimants, the great majority of whom are not domiciled in Poland and are not Polish citizens. In the absence of legislation, no mechanism yet exists that would provide for the return of private assets and the matter continues to be the subject of national and international debate.

Populist, nationalist and antisemitic parties and right-wing parties with far right connections won some 40 percent of the vote in the September 2001 parliamentary elections. The Liga Polskich Rodzin (LPR) became the first party of the antisemitic extreme right in postwar Polish history to gain seats in parliament (40 out of 460; 7 percent of the vote). The party was formed shortly before the election on the initiative of Father Tadeusz Rydzyk, founder and director of the Catholic nationalist Radio Maryja, the main disseminator of antisemitic propaganda in Poland, which attracts about 4 percent of Polish society as regular listeners. The populist Samoobrona party, which has been trying to distance itself from its far right past, won 10 percent of the vote. However, the attendance of Nazi skinheads at the party's election meetings indicates that links with the far right have not been cut completely.

Among extremist extra-parliamentary groups, perhaps the most dynamic is Narodowe Odrodzenie Polski (NOP), which claims to be an incarnation of the pre-war Oboz Narodowo-Radykalny, banned by the Polish government in 1934. The antisemitic culture which dominates many sports stadiums in Poland is fertile recruiting ground for the NOP. Party leader Adam Gmurczyk is openly antisemitic, asserting: "Europe was great, it was Christian – because it was antisemitic... antisemitism is the virtue that we must cultivate with great care." The NOP subscribes to the Catholic fundamentalist ideology of Bishop Marcel Lefebvre (who repudiated the 1965 Vatican II Council reforms) and denies the Holocaust. The NOP has sympathizers in other countries, notably among the US Polish community, including organizations such as the New York-based Polish Patriots' Association and the Chicago-based revisionist Polish Historical Institute.

The number of antisemitic incidents remained relatively high in 2001 and 2002. Some incidents may be attributed to the increase in antisemitic propaganda in the wake of the Jedwabne debate (see below). A fire, which broke out at the museum on the site of the former concentration camp Majdanek on 19 May 2001 was suspected of being an arson attack. Similarly, police suspect that a fire in the synagogue at Breslau on 10 May 2002 may have been arson. Two days previously thirty-nine tombstones in the Jewish cemetery of Oswiecim (Auschwitz) were overturned and smeared with antisemitic slogans and swastikas.

Extreme nationalists and antisemites, including members of parliament, continued their campaign against commemoration of the 1941 Jedwabne massacre (see http://www.tau.ac.il/Anti-Semitism/asw2001-2/wistrich.htm). A leading activist in this campaign, LPR founder and head Ryszard Bender, accused President Aleksander Kwasniewski, who took part in the official ceremony marking the event in July 2001, of serving Jewish interest groups. Another well known antisemite involved in the campaign is Leszek Bubel, head of the marginal Polska Partia Narodowa (Polish National Party), who is greeted as a folk hero by antisemitic inhabitants in Jedwabne today. The participation of President Aleksander Kwasniewski in the official ceremony was an important step in Polish acknowledgment of responsibility for the event.

According to the preliminary results of the Romanian census published in July 2002, the Jewish community in Romania has dwindled to less than 6,000 out of a total population of 21.5 million. The major Jews centers are Bucharest, Iasi, Cluj and Oradea, where the local communities are well organized. The Federation of Jewish Communities of Romania promotes and coordinates their activities. The issue of restitution of private and communal property has still to be resolved in Romania, although the community has secured the return of several individual items.

There was one incidence of vandalism in 2001 when 20 gravestones were smashed in the Jewish cemetery of Zalau in September, and there were two incidents of synagogue desecration in 2002. A direct link between antisemitic activity in 2001 and the first half of 2002 and the electoral achievements of the Greater Romania Party (PRM) in late 2000 (see *ASW 2000/1*) could not be proven.

Several antisemitic works appeared in 2001. *The Nationalist*, by PRM deputy Vlad Hogea, a collection of articles originally published in the PRM organ *Romania Mare* and issued under the auspices of a research institute affiliated with the Romanian Academy of Sciences, was being investigated by the judicial authorities for antisemitic and racist (anti-Roma and anti-Hungarian) content. In response to the public controversy aroused by this work, an article in *Romania Mare* (25 Aug. 2001) branded the Federation of Jewish Communities in Romania "a state within a state" and denied there was antisemitism in Romania, aside from that caused by Jewish elements, which had brought communism and were continuing to "torture" that innocent nation. Another antisemitic work, *In Search of the Lost Legion*, by Razvan Codrescu, was published with the support of the Ministry of Culture and Religion. These examples, as well as the open display of antisemitic literature at bookstores in major cities, indicate that despite official attempts to ban it and to educate the public against racism and antisemitism, such works are being published and distributed even under the auspices of academic and government agencies.

There was a notable increase in the number of websites linked to the Romanian extreme right, especially to the Iron Guard, which appears to parallel the expansion of the Internet in Romania

Following the September 11 events, the PRM initially printed allegations, based on foreign sources, that Israelis and Jews "had been warned" a day before the attacks. However, it modified its tone after deciding to support the war on terror. In its ongoing slander campaign against former Jewish communists and against Israeli and Jewish businessmen in Romania, the PRM focused less than in previous years on alleged Israeli-Jewish-US hegemonic policies in the global arena, but it continued and even intensified its denial of the Holocaust of Romanian Jews.

Despite steps taken by the government, as well as by state and public institutions, to ban Holocaust denial and to clamp down on the Antonescu cult, especially in 2001/2 (including "emergency measures" issued on 21 March 2002 to ban racist, fascist and xenophobic organizations as well as monuments honoring people guilty of crimes against humanity, and to protect Jewish heritage sites and cemeteries), revisionist elements were far from being suppressed. For example, while several busts of Antonescu were removed and streets renamed, Gheorghe Funar, a leading PRM member and mayor of Cluj, responded to pressure from the authorities by moving a bust of the wartime fascist leader to a less conspicuous place.

During 2001/2 the debate in Romanian society on the nation's role in the Holocaust intensified, with arguments for and against the rehabilitation of Antonescu and the fate of Romanian Jewry being clearly linked to Romania's attempts to enter NATO, the EU and other structures of European integration. In the public discourse, semantics and ad hoc attempts to define or redefine terms such as the "Holocaust" often led to confusion and contradictions. Thus, at a conference organized by the Romanian Academy of Sciences in late June 2002, "The Holocaust and Its Implications for Romania," Minister of Culture Razvan Theodorescu considered that "Romania had nothing to do with the Holocaust, but, under the Antonescu regime and following the occupation of territories beyond the River Dniestr, Romania participated in the Holocaust" (*Rompress*, 28 June, 2002).

During 2001/2 there were numerous responses to antisemitism and discussions on the implications of the past on the present and future of the country. Prime Minister Adrian Nastase emphasized several times that Romania should assume responsibility for the past; however, differences of opinion remain between the official Romanian position and Western historians and the Jewish world on the extent of the Holocaust in Romania.

Slovakia has some 3,000 Jews out of a total population of 5.35 million. The largest Jewish community is in the capital Bratislava; smaller communities exist in Kosice, Presov, Komarno and Dunajska Sreda. The Central Union of Jewish Religious Communities in the Slovak Republic is the main communal organization. In 2002 the Central Union reached an agreement with the Slovak government on the formation of a commission which would examine the issue of compensation for Holocaust victims.

There were several incidents of Jewish cemetery desecration in 2001/2. Some 50 tombstones were damaged in Levice, southern Slovakia, and seven were destroyed in Vranov nad Toplou, eastern Slovakia. Eleven tombstones were also vandalized in the old Jewish cemetery of Zvolen at the end of June 2001.One hundred and thirty-five graves in the Jewish cemetery at Kosice were found desecrated on 21 April 2002.

Rehabilitation of the wartime Tiso regime continued to be the main theme of the struggle in 2001/2, between neo-fascist, antisemitic and populist elements, and liberal forces. Pro-Tiso supporters carried out provocative acts which were widely reported in the media and placed the issue of rehabilitation on the agenda of the September 2002 elections. For example, right-wing extremists marked the 62nd anniversary of the wartime state with a meeting at Tiso's grave at the Martin cemetery in Bratislava and an authorized demonstration attended by neo-fascists and skinheads in front of the presidential offices in Bratislava.

The attempts to rewrite history and rehabilitate the wartime ideological line continued in a variety of forums.. In 2001 the proceedings of a seminar held in 1998 honoring Karol Sidor, founder of the notorious fascist Hlinka Guard, which played a major role in anti-Jewish activities in Slovakia before 1939, were published. Also in 2001, revisionist Milan S. Durica (see *ASW 1999/2000, 2000/1*) edited and published a volume, *The Catholic Church in Slovakia 1938–1945 as Viewed by German Diplomats and Secret Agents*. The book alleges not only that Tiso's regime and the Church had nothing to do with fascism and the Holocaust, but that it in fact saved the majority of Jews.

The Slovak Catholic Church also supports preserving the memory of Tiso in a positive light. Its position is reflected in the memoirs of the nonagenarian Catholic priest Viktor Trstensky, who was persecuted in the communist period and rehabilitated in 1990. The book, *Further*

Painful Outpourings of a Soul Longing for Truth and Justice, which echoes the spirit of Tiso and the Slovak fascist state, contains antisemitic passages.

Government promises and actions (such as President Rudolf Schuster's declaration of 9 September as a memorial day for victims of the Holocaust and of racial violence – see *ASW 2000/1*) have done little to weaken the trend of historical revisionism.

The September 2002 elections were a severe test for the troubled coalition government of pro-European parties, led by Mikulos Dzurinda, which had survived numerous internal conflicts and parliamentary no-confidence motions. Slovakia's attempts to join NATO and the European Union have continued to serve as a prime strategic objective, influencing the country's policy on minority issues.

The Middle East

Developments in the year 2001 provided fertile ground for Arab Islamic antisemitism. The intifada continued to be a major pretext for incitement against Israel and the Jews, although the wave of antisemitic manifestations which typified the period after its eruption in September 2000 receded. On the other hand, the September 11 events triggered a rise in antisemitic allegations and exposed the linkage between anti-Americanism and antisemitism in the Arab world. Although it is difficult to assess antisemitic manifestations in the Arab world quantitatively, the trend toward radicalizing the discourse on Israel and the Jews, discerned following the outbreak of the intifada (see *ASW 2000/1*) continued. Moreover, it seemed to spread beyond political and journalistic debates. Apart from the imminent threat to Jews worldwide as part of the Islamists' war against the West and particularly the US, revealed in the September 11 events, this radicalization was manifested in several ways:
- Crude attacks – intertwined with antisemitic allusions – on newly-elected prime minister of Israel Ariel Sharon (February 2001);
- Popularization of antisemitic motifs, such as the blood libel and the Jewish conspiracy to control the world;
- Equating Zionism with racism and Nazism in the struggle against Israel in international forums;
- Embracing Holocaust denial as a means of delegitimizing Israel and Zionism;
- Sanctioning suicide attacks against Israeli civilian targets as well as attacks on Jewish targets worldwide.

The September 11 attacks on the World Trade Center in New York and the Pentagon in Washington by a group of radical Islamists instigated a wave of antisemitic manifestations. Usama bin Ladin and the Islamists brought about Islamization of the anti-American and anti-imperialist polemic in the same way that the intifada reinforced Islamization of the Arab-Israeli conflict and the anti-Israel discourse. Hostility toward the Jews and Israel is part and parcel of the worldview of bin Ladin and al-Qa'ida (the base) as well as of other Islamist movements, such as Hamas and Islamic Jihad. The struggle, or jihad, against "the Crusaders and the Jews" is a major theme in bin Ladin's ideology and constitutes the first stage in a long campaign for the restoration of the Muslim caliphate and the establishment of an Islamic world order. According to this view, the Jews are not only the occupiers of Muslim lands in Palestine but are part of Western Judeo-Christian civilization, perceived as a threat to Islamic civilization and Islamic revival. Although seen also as the spearhead of the West in the war against Islam, the Jews and the issue of the Arab-Israeli conflict were not bin Ladin's first priority. Only when he felt during America's retaliatory war in Afghanistan that the Arab and Muslim demonstrations against the US were waning did he raise the Palestinian cause to the top of the agenda in his video addresses urging Muslims to action.

North America

CANADA

Canada's Jewish population in 2001 was estimated at 364,000 out of a total population of 31 million. Most of the community is divided between Toronto and Montreal, with other major centers in Vancouver, Winnipeg and Ottawa. B'nai B'rith Canada and the Canadian Jewish Congress are the two major national Jewish advocacy organizations. The community publishes some 20 newspapers and journals, including *The Jewish Tribune* and the *Canadian Jewish News*.

In total, 286 antisemitic incidents were reported to the League for Human Rights in 2001, roughly the same level as in 2000, but an increase of 7 percent over the pre-intifada level in 1999. Thirty-five percent of all incidents were recorded in the wake of 11 September, 20 percent in the immediate aftermath and close to an additional 15 percent in October. In Quebec, the number of antisemitic incidents rose by 11 percent in 2001, and a new attitudinal survey suggested that there was a higher level of prejudice in Quebec toward Jews than in the rest of Canada.

The Jewish community suffered bomb threats, anthrax scares, physical assaults on individuals, vandalism of synagogues and community institutions, cemetery desecrations, harassment and hate propaganda. Pro-Palestinian demonstrations in Canada also had antisemitic features. The "Zionism equals Racism" canard re-appeared on the streets of Canada, particularly after the widespread dissemination of such propaganda at the UN-sponsored World Conference against Racism in Durban in September 2001.

White supremacist and neo-Nazi activity has decreased in Canada over the past decade. Nevertheless, racist groups from the United States, such as William Pierce's white supremacist National Alliance, have reportedly been active in Canada, and a number of locally-based groups operate websites. The Canadian Ethnic Cleansing Team was the focus of attention due to an Internet newsletter it posted after the September 11 attacks, which included a threat to "B'nai B'rith offices, Mossad temples and any Jew [or] Arab Temple, building, house and cars. There are no innocent Jews especially in a time of war."

The university campus continued to be a source of antisemitic propaganda and the number of incidents targeting Jewish college students increased. It is particularly noticeable on campus that hegemony over antisemitism appears to have shifted from white supremacists to groups propagating the myth that not just Israel, but also Jews, should be blamed for the current conflict in the Middle East, the events of 11 September and most of the ills of the world. A leading university in this regard is Concordia, where the student union is dominated by Arabs/Muslims and left-wingers/anti-globalization supporters.

Before the September 11 events the Canadian Security Intelligence Services (CSIS) reported that they were monitoring more than 50 terrorist groups – including Hamas, Hizballah, Islamic Jihad and al-Qaʻida –as well as 350 operatives. New anti-terrorism legislation introduced in 2001 seeks to prevent groups connected with terrorist activities from functioning, recruiting and fundraising in Canada. Amendments were also added to the Criminal Code to create a new offense of crimes against places of religious worship or religious property, and to the Human Rights Act, extending the prohibition against hate messages to include all telecommunication technologies, including the Internet.

The Jewish community in the United States constitutes the largest concentration of Jews in the world, numbering 5.2 million and comprising 1.8 percent of the total population of 281.4 million. The bulk of American Jewry lives in major cities and their environs, including New York City, Los Angeles, Southeast Florida, Chicago, Boston, San Francisco, Philadelphia and Cleveland. Leading national Jewish organizations include the American Israel Public Affairs Committee (AIPAC), American Jewish Committee, American Jewish Congress, American Jewish Joint Distribution Committee (JDC), Anti-Defamation League (ADL), B'nai B'rith, Hadassah, Zionist Organization of America (ZOA) and Jewish War Veterans (JWV). A merger between the Council of Jewish Federations, United Israel Appeal and United Jewish Appeal in 1998 created the United Jewish Communities (UJC), which represents Jewish community federations and independent Jewish communities throughout North America.

The total number of antisemitic incidents in 2001 decreased from the year 2000. Forty states and the District of Columbia reported 1,434 antisemitic incidents, marking a fall of 172 incidents below the 2000 total of 1,606. This represents an 11 percent decrease in anti-Jewish activity, reversing the upward trend prior to 2001, which saw a 4 percent increase. As in the past, harassment directed at individuals and institutions made up more than half of all incidents reported (approximately 61 percent); 556 acts of vandalism were recorded – the lowest total in 20 years. Higher security awareness by Jewish communal institutions and significant law enforcement mobilization since 11 September may have accounted for the substantial decrease of antisemitic vandalism incidents.

Among the worst antisemitic incidents were a shooting and a bomb threat directed at a synagogue in Des Moines, Iowa; a synagogue arson attack in Tacoma, Washington, and a cemetery desecration in Greensburg, Pennsylvania.

The Ku Klux Klan, World Church of the Creator, National Alliance, Christian Identity groups and others continue to canvass neighborhoods with their racist propaganda. In addition, in the wake of 11 September, there was a convergence between American right- and left-wing extremists – who have long exploited currents events, particularly in the Middle East, to blame America's troubles on Jews, Israel and American foreign policy – and extremist Arabs and Muslims (see *General Analysis*).

A striking outgrowth of extremist exploitation of the Internet is the attempt of hate groups to capitalize on the popularity of computer video games – especially among teens – by manipulating technology to create violently racist and antisemitic versions of popular games. Games with titles such as "Ethnic Cleansing" and "Shoot the Blacks" may be previewed, purchased and downloaded from the websites of some of the nation's most dangerous neo-Nazi, white supremacist and Holocaust denial groups.

The California-based Institute for Historical Review (IHR), the most active Holocaust denying organization in the US, planned to hold its annual conference in 2001 in Beirut, in cooperation with the Swiss-based Vérité et Justice. However, they were forced to cancel the conference due to pressure from Jewish and other organizations (see http://www.tau.ac.il/Anti-Semitism/asw2001-2/arab.htm).

Latin America

ARGENTINA

With about 200,000 Jews out of a total population of over 35 million, Argentina has the largest Jewish community in Latin America. The great majority of Jews live in Buenos Aires and its environs; however, there are also sizable communities in Rosario, Córdoba and Santa Fe. The leading Jewish organization is DAIA (Delegación de Asociaciones Israelitas Argentinas), which represents communities and organizations to the authorities and is responsible for safeguarding the rights of members. AMIA (Asociación Mutual Israelita Argentina) is the main community organization. The Vaad ha-Kehilot is the umbrella organization of all the communities in the provinces.

In recent years the economic situation of Jews in Argentina has deteriorated severely, particularly in the wake of the collapse of Jewish banks, and ultimately of the entire economy. In January 2002 at an assembly convoked by the DAIA, with the participation of representatives of all its institutions, the Argentinean Jewish community declared itself in a state of emergency. There has been a dramatic rise in the number of applications for aliya, as well as for emigration to other parts of the world, notably Spanish-speaking countries in Central America as well as Spain.

The number and nature of antisemitic manifestations remained relatively unchanged in 2001, with 172 incidents, compared to 177 in 2000 and 166 in 1999. A Jewish musician in Buenos Aires was badly injured in a mail bomb explosion in April. The cover of the box he opened was adorned with a swastika and the letters SS. Further, a month before its re-dedication in September 2001, police received five anonymous calls threatening to blow up the reconstructed AMIA building again.

Antisemitism appears mainly in publications of the extreme right. The mainstream media may be critical of Israeli policy but since the attacks on the Israeli embassy and the AMIA building it has been careful to avoid expressions that might be interpreted as antisemitic. After 11 September, some articles of the far right that attacked the US and its association with Israel contained anti-Zionist and antisemitic references.

Among nationalist, extreme right journals that print virulently antisemitic material, the traditionalist Catholic *Cabildo* attacked the DAIA (in the context of a debate in Catamarca province about the controversial issue of compulsory religious education) for its lack of respect for the Catholic religion and asserted that the Catholic religion must be defended against the Jewish community. In 2000/1 it published articles identifying with Holocaust deniers such as David Irving (UK), and Robert Garaudy and Robert Faurisson (France). The journal also blames the Jews for the adoption of Argentina's anti-discrimination law.

The oral public trial of 20 persons accused of bombing the AMIA building in 1994 failed to throw light on the chain of events that led up to the attack because of the obstructionist tactics of local police officers. In July 2002, the *New York Times* revealed that former President Carlos Menem had received a large sum of money from Iran in order to hinder the investigation of the AMIA bombing. The matter is being investigated by the Argentinean judicial authorities.

The case against legalizing the neo-Nazi Partido Neuvo Triunfo (PNT) and the Partido Nuevo Orden Social (PNOSP) is continuing. The government has asked the Justice Ministry not to legalize these parties, because they "incite to violence and antisemitic hatred" and vindicate Hitler, and their ideology is anti-democratic.

Brazil, the largest country in Latin America, has a Jewish population of about 110,000, out of a total population of over 160 million inhabitants. Most of the Jews live in Brazil's major cities – Río de Janeiro, São Paulo and Porto Alegre – but some live in small communities on the shores of the Amazon River and in other remote locations, such as Bahia, Belém and Manaus. The central body representing all the Jewish federations and communities in Brazil is the Confederação Israelita do Brasil (CONIB), founded in 1951.

Brazil experienced a growth in antisemitic activity, mainly IN propaganda, in 2001, triggered largely by anti-Zionist and anti-American expressions after 11 September. A few incidents of vandalism were recorded, including the tearing of mezzuzahs from two synagogues. Anti-Jewish slogans were scrawled on the walls of Jewish facilities in Porto Alegre in February, and the wall of a Jewish home in Rio de Janeiro was painted with swastikas and abusive slogans on the night of Hitler's birthday, 20–21 April.

Brazil has the largest number of antisemitic websites in South America. Comments such as "Hitler was right," "Germany was right," "Israel must suffer an atom bomb attack and disappear forever," and "Nazi Sharon and Nazi Israelis must be tortured to death" were reported in chat and discussion forums on the Israeli-Palestinian conflict (such as the Terra server's news forum *Medium Orient*). A new server, Cosmo On-Line, claiming to be the voice of the state of São Paulo, and providing daily news on the Palestinian question, disseminates anti-Israel articles by pro-Palestinian Brazilian intellectuals and Arab experts, such as the piece "Nazisrael" by Professor José Arbex, who accused Sharon of promoting genocide.

The September 11 attacks and their aftermath, particularly the American attack on Afghanistan, sparked an increase in anti-American expressions of leading Brazilian public figures, such as Judge Fabio Konder Comparato and Milton Temer (see *General Analysis*). Anti-American opinions were also expressed by Muslim leaders, such as the São Paulo Muslim cleric of Lebanese descent Salah Sleiman, who translated a sermon of Egyptian Muslim cleric Mustafa Shukri Ismail, which claimed there was a war between the two cultures (Islamic and Western), one spiritual and pure, the other greedy and immoral.

Occasionally, criticism of American policy was coupled with anti-Zionist rhetoric and attacks on Israel. Philosopher José Arthur Giannotti claimed that the creation of Israel had caused deep wounds in the relationship between the Arabs and the Western world, which had to be dealt with before terrorism could be eliminated.

Some openly antisemitic critics depicted Israel as the ultimate evil and equated Israel with Nazi Germany. For example, the mainstream publications *Correio Brasiliense*, on 14 April, and *O Globo*, on 1 May 2002, published a cartoon showing the devil sitting at a table with a flag bearing the Star of David in the background. During anti-Israel demonstrations held on 4 and 5 April 2002 in São Paulo, 400–500 participants, mostly radical Muslims and leftists, shouted antisemitic slogans, such as "The Jews are not part of the human race..." and "Hitler was a pupil of the Jews" and waved placards displaying swastikas and equating Israeli Prime Minister Ariel Sharon with Hitler.

According to Ilanud (Instituto Latino Americano das Nações Unidas para a Prevenção do Delito e o Tratamento do Delinqüente), more than 30 *carecas* (roughly, skinhead) groups are active in Brazil (especially in São Paulo and Rio de Janeiro), with a total of 1,000 members. Like their counterparts in Europe, the creed of many of them includes neo-Nazism, antisemitism and xenophobia, and almost all are homophobic.

A petition, signed by 100 Jewish and non-Jewish intellectuals demanding that the books of Editora Revisão publishing house, owned by the convicted Holocaust denier and antisemite Sigfried Ellwanger, be banned from display at the Porto Alegre book fair, was rejected by the president of the Rio Grande do Sul Book Association. In 2002 Ellwanger's appeal before the Federal Supreme Court that he could not be accused of racism because the Jews were not a race, was accepted and he was acquitted.

The Jewish community of Chile, numbering approximately 21,000 out of a total population of 14.5 million, is mostly concentrated in the city of Santiago de Chile, with a scattering in the provinces of Valparaíso, Viña del Rancagua, Concepción, Temuco and Valdivia. The Representative Committee of Jewish Organizations in Chile (CREJ) encompasses all the Jewish communities and organizations in the country.

The violence in the Middle East and the resurgence of pro-Palestinian activities in Chile seem to have instigated a larger number and a more serious type of violent actions than in previous years. Chilean Jews experienced several violent incidents in the course of 2001. In April, human excrement was thrown at a kosher restaurant in Santiago and a stone was flung at the Jewish firefighters' association Bomba de Israel, smashing a window. On 3 June young Jews sitting in two fast-food restaurants in Santiago were assaulted by a group of Palestinians in their early twenties, who wore kaffiyehs and leather jackets and carried chains. Several phone and e-mail threats were received by Jewish organizations. For instance, two phone calls, one in March to the Estadio Israelita building and the other in May to the Instituto Hebreo school, threatened harm to children.

After the eruption of the second intifada in September 2000, the 300,000-strong Palestinian community worked vigorously, using the weight of its numbers and status within the country, to place the Palestinian cause on the Chilean public agenda. In 2001 the level of activity and cooperation of the various groups was unprecedented and their tone was extremely anti-Israel and often antisemitic. Congressman Eugenio Tuma Zedán, a member of the center-left party Partido Popular Democratico, for example, asked the Ministry of Defense, on behalf of the Palestinian community, in early September 2001, to investigate the continuous presence of Israeli youth in Pumalin Park, a popular tourist attraction. He also asked for an inquiry into Zionist activities in Chile and questioned whether they were legal in light of Zionist "racist" practices.

Some of the Palestinian groups promote antisemitism. The Asociacíon de jóvenes por Palestina website, for example, has a game called "Biting the Jewish mouse." The Union General de Estudiantes Palestinos transmits a weekly radio program "Palestine Forever," with anti-Israel, anti-Zionist and antisemitic messages. The Federacíon Palestina de Chile holds masses in memory of suicide bombers and prays for an end to the "Palestinian holocaust." In an interview to the independent periodical *la Hora*, distributed free-of-charge, in February, Eugenio Chachauan, director of the Centro de Estudios Arabes de la Universidad de Chile, claimed that since "the Jews murdered the Messiah they can be expected to murder anyone."

Although the Muslim community in Chile numbers no more than 3,000 there was some anti-Muslim sentiment after the September 11 events. Some Chilean Islamists are suspected of links to the Lebanese Hizballah and to international terrorist activity in the northern city of Iquique, bordering Peru and Bolivia.

The leading neo-Nazi group Movimiento Patria Nueva Sociedad (PNS), led by Alexis López Tapia, has been attempting to create regional cells, probably with the aim of becoming a political party. Its Internet page was the center of the group's activity in 2001. Erwin Robertson, leader of the ultra-right-wing, nationalist Revista Ciudad de los Césares, published a book in 2001 entitled *Se Acabó Chile* (Chile Is Finished), in which he claims that the Jews dominate everything and everywhere.

The Jewish community in Mexico numbers about 40,000, out of a total population of 102 million. Most Jews live in the capital Mexico City and its suburbs, while the rest are located in the cities of Guadalajara, Monterrey, Tijuana, and in Cancún. The main communities, together with the Jewish Sports Center, are represented in the Jewish Central Committee of Mexico (JCCM). Tribuna Israelita, the community's public opinion and analysis agency, promotes an ongoing dialogue with opinion leaders and implements joint projects with various national organizations.

Most antisemitism in Mexico in 2001 was expressed in anonymous letters and graffiti, and in printed and Internet propaganda. Jewish institutions received anonymous antisemitic mail continuously throughout the year. They included abuse such as: "Jewish pigs, Mexico is for the Mexicans... Get the hell out of our country"; "I support Yasir Arafat. I hope he will get rid of you"; and "I'm sorry Hitler didn't finish you off." In addition, anti-Jewish graffiti appeared in suburbs of Mexico City with large Jewish populations, as well as at UNAM University, and anti-Jewish leaflets were found in phone booths in the Condesa quarter of the city.

Propaganda of the Mexican extreme right was disseminated on the Internet via the Argentinean neo-Nazi site of Alejandro Biondini. Groups promoting the country's Creole identity, such as Orgullo Criollo and Partido Nacional Socialista de Mexico, which consider themselves part of a white Mexican supremacist movement, blame the Jews for the problems of Mexico and of the world.

The Israeli-Palestinian conflict generated a significant number of anti-Israel and anti-Zionist articles in the national media. Israel was portrayed as a militaristic and violent nation whose attitude toward the Palestinians was racial and genocidal. "Israel was created and is maintained through terrorist actions against the Palestinians," asserted one commentator in the leftist newspaper *La Jornada* (6 Dec.). Letters to the editor claimed, for example, that "Sharon is a murderer, a butcher who defends imperialism in the Middle East. Long live the intifada!" and, "Israel... has been and will always be ungrateful to Mexico... Being Jews, different from the rest, they abuse the Palestinians, in revenge for the Russian and Polish pogroms and the Holocaust" (Augusto Hugo Peña, in *Excelsior*, 28 Nov.).

Members of the Jewish community participated in the Anti-discrimination Commission created by President Vicente Fox. The draft of an anti-discrimination law presented to the president by the commission in November declares that antisemitism and xenophobia constitute discriminatory behavior.

The Jewish community of Uruguay is estimated at about 25,000 out of a total population of 3.2 million. The majority of Jews live in the capital Montevideo, with a smaller community in the city of Paysandú. The Comité Central Israelita del Uruguay (CCIU), embracing some 60 communities and organizations, functions as the national Jewish representative body.

Although antisemitism remained on the same level as in 2000, there were some troubling manifestations previously unknown in Uruguay linked to the Israeli-Palestinian conflict. These included anti-Jewish slogans during anti-Israel demonstrations outside the Israeli embassy in Montevideo and antisemitic content in pamphlets concerning the conflict.

There were two minor acts of vandalism in Montevideo: a stone thrown in December at the residence of a Jewish woman, and a swastika daubed on the car of Jewish individual, as well as several phone threats. In addition, there were reports of anti-Jewish graffiti in some suburbs of Montevideo. Offensive e-mail messages were received by several Jewish individuals, and staff at Jewish institutions reported receiving virus-infected e-mail decorated with an eagle and swastikas.

The Uruguayan public appears to be relatively indifferent to the Israeli-Palestinian conflict. A survey conducted in the leading newspaper *El Observador* (18 Nov.) asked, *inter alia*, with whom readers identified more, Ariel Sharon or Yasir Arafat. Nineteen percent stated Sharon and 16 percent, Arafat; the rest had no opinion.

Venezuela's Jewish community numbers about 22,000 out of a total population of nearly 22 million. Most Jews live in the capital Caracas, while the second largest community is located in Maracaíbo. The Confederación de Asociaciones Israelitas de Venezuela (CAIV) embraces four organizations: Asociación Israelita de Venezuela (Sephardi), Unión Israelita de Caracas (Ashkenazi), the Zionist Organization and B'nai B'rith.

While the number of antisemitic incidents remained on the same level as the previous year, there was a notable rise in anti-Zionist expressions, which were often mixed with antisemitic threats and insults during the polemic on the Israeli-Palestinian conflict. There were no violent antisemitic actions in 2001, but seven death threat calls were received at Jewish community institutions. Three were made in September to the Moral y Luces Herzl-Bialik school. They said, "Everyone will die"; "We shall take a break but at the end we will get rid of you all and your cursed school. Happy Yom Kippur"; and "We know that it is Yom Kippur and we shall murder all the children when they leave the school." Antisemitic placards appeared in the city, especially in the Central University of Venezuela, and threat letters containing antisemitic slogans and swastikas were placed on cars owned by Jews. A rise in the use of Nazi symbols and expressions was noted.

The line between anti-Israel/anti-Zionist and antisemitic rhetoric was often blurred. This trend was marked at several discussion forums held during 2001. On 6 December 2001 a conference was held by the Comite Nacional Marcha hacia el Muro por la Paz, la Justicia Social y contra el Neoliberalismo, entitled "A Condemnation of the State Terror of the Zionist and Imperialist State." The conference was financed by public sources and attended by government officials, as well as by 20 members of foreign diplomatic delegations in Venezuela.

Several articles appeared in the national press which compared Israeli conduct toward the Palestinians with Nazi behavior toward the Jews. Further, numerous articles published in mainstream papers throughout Venezuela during 2001 branded Israeli Prime Minister Ariel Sharon a terrorist, who massacred Palestinians and violated human rights.

After the September 11 events, articles and letters in the mainstream press blamed US support of Israel and the Jews for sowing the seeds of hatred against it. The US attack in Afghanistan was branded terrorism and compared to Israel's attacks on Palestinians (for more on this subject, see *General Analysis*). The Internet site of the Mosque of Caracas, which hitherto had not participated in the discourse on the Israeli-Palestinian conflict, disseminated an article which claimed: "The first terrorism is that of the Jewish nation, a nation of anger that America is defending in the name of justice and injustice by aiding them militarily, economically and politically; this is the real terrorism."

Australia and South Africa

AUSTRALIA

The 115–120,000 Jews in Australia out of a total population of 17,850,000 comprise the largest Jewish community in the East Asia Pacific Region. The great majority of Australian Jews live in Melbourne and Sydney, but there are also significant communities in Perth, Brisbane, the Gold Coast and Adelaide. The leading communal organization is the Executive Council of Australian Jewry (ECAJ).

The November 2001 federal election was held against the backdrop of Australia's participation in the US-led war against terrorism and a public debate on the issue of how Australia should respond to the arrival of asylum seekers, applicants for refugee status and persons without documents who apply to remain in Australia. The tough stand by the main political parties on both these issues was largely interpreted as being the reason the right-wing populist party One Nation failed to have any of its candidates elected to either the Senate or the House of Representatives. The total vote for parties of the antisemitic right-wing fringe was extremely negligible.

Although the many small groups which comprise the Australian far left often make declarations critical of racism in all its forms, demonization of Israel is a common thread and the language used to condemn Zionism and Israel are almost indistinguishable from that of the far right. Trotskyist or pro-communist groups, for example, regularly proclaim their opposition to antisemitism but use antisemitic language when discussing Israel.

Antisemitic elements within the Arabic-speaking and Islamic communities often draw on the same material as white supremacists, "Identity" groups and other overt racists, and vice-versa. Material from extreme right-wing sources was published on the web pages of the West Australian Islamic Network, while antisemitic New-Age conspiracy theorist William Cooper's interpretation of the World Trade Center attacks was published on the site of the Federation of Australian Muslims and Youth (FAMSY).

In total, 328 reports of antisemitic violence, vandalism, harassment and intimidation were logged during 2001, the third highest on record. The number of incidents of violence and property damage exceeded by 50 per cent the previous highest tally (1996) and was over double the annual average. In-your-face harassment was reported at its second highest level and one-third above the average. At least six individuals were physically assaulted, and synagogues were stoned or petrol bombed in NSW, Tasmania, the ACT and Western Australia.

The year 2001 saw a dramatic increase in articles, commentaries and letters in mainstream papers which made explicit or implicit anti-Jewish statements, in most cases related to events in the Middle East or to 11 September. One letter claimed that Australia was safe from terrorism unless the government took "orders from the US and the Jewish lobby."

In September 2002 the Federal Court upheld complaints of antisemitism and Holocaust denial lodged by the ECAJ against Olga Scully and Adelaide Institute head Fredrick Toben. It ordered both Scully and Toben to desist from distributing literature offensive to Jews.

The state governments of Queensland and Victoria both enacted comprehensive legislation designed to give victims of racial and religious vilification and intolerance a measure of legal recourse, which now means all Australian states and territories have such statutes.

South Africa has the largest Jewish community on the African continent, numbering approximately 85,000 out of a total population of some 43 million. Most Jews live in Johannesburg and Cape Town; other centers are Durban and Pretoria. The Jewish community has been in steady decline, a result of the political uncertainty and increasing violence that characterized the last two decades of minority white rule, as well as compulsory military service for white males. The South African Jewish Board of Deputies (SAJBD), a recognized civil rights organization, *inter alia*, monitors levels of antisemitism in the country and takes action where necessary.

Despite a pronounced rise in antisemitic sentiment, largely as a result of the ongoing violence in the Middle East and the fact that South Africa was the host country for the World Conference against Racism (see below), the number of antisemitic incidents reported overall in 2001, as in previous years, was low. The most serious instance of antisemitic violence took place in September when an elderly Jewish doctor in Cape Town was assaulted in his rooms by three men wearing keffiyahs. The assailants reportedly told the doctor: "You Jews are the ones making trouble in the Middle East."

During 2001, Israel came under attack in South Africa as never before, both in the media and at government level. At times the line between criticism of Israel and antisemitism became blurred. The African National Council's (ANC) pro-Palestinian stance became increasingly overt, with comparisons between the Palestinian-Israeli conflict and the fight against apartheid becoming common currency. Even more extreme were leftist parties, such as the Congress of South African Trade Unions, the South African Communist Party, the Azanian People's Organisation and the Pan African Congress. These mainly black-supported groupings vied with one another in issuing statements delegitimizing Israel and calling for South Africa and the international community to turn it into a pariah state. In August Mazibuko Jara, a spokesperson for the SACP, requested an audience with the minister of foreign affairs. He claimed the purpose of the meeting was to discuss allegations that the South African Jewish community was "financially assisting the Israeli government to suppress the Palestinian people."

The World Conference against Racism (WCAR), which took place in Durban from 27 August to 9 September, demonstrated the strength and capabilities of local Muslim groups in South Africa, which were able to coordinate their activities with international organizations and states on a number of levels. Islamist groups active at the conference were the Muslim Judicial Foundation, Ahlul Bait Foundation and the Media Review Network, which organized a pro-Palestinian demonstration on 21 August at which some 20,000 Muslims and supporters were whipped into a frenzy of anti-Jewish emotion, including calls of "Jews are the scum of the earth." (For more on the conference, see *General Analysis*.)

Numerous anti-Israel rallies at which antisemitic expressions were heard as well, took place countrywide during the course of the year, notably in the period of the WCAR and after the 11 September attacks. At an al-Quds Day rally in Cape Town in December, Qibla founder Ahmed Cassim, said "What was seen as the final solution for the Jews in the Diaspora, that is, the creation of the Zionist Terrorist State of Israel, has become its worst nightmare and possibly its final nightmare."

Overt antisemitism in the press usually took the form of readers' letters. Following the September 11 attacks and America's military campaign against the Taliban, a large number of extremely anti-Israel letters, frequently with antisemitic overtones, appeared in the Muslim and general press. For example on 13 October the *Eastern Province Herald* published a reader's letter which identified the Jews with the US government and accused "the Jews" of having "killed millions of people the world over." It should be pointed out that not since the 1930s has such an anti-Jewish attack appeared in a respectable mainstream publication in South Africa. Following a complaint by the SAJBD, the editor of the paper noted that Campbell's letter had been published in order to expose the depth of extreme anti-American and anti-Jewish feeling in South Africa

There were clear parallels between antisemitism in *Die Afrikaner*, organ of the far right Herstigte Nasionale Party, and that emanating from sectors of the Muslim community, suggesting that the two groups were influencing each other. For example, a lengthy two-part article, published in the 12 and 19 October issues of *Die Afrikaner*, hinted at similarities between the Pearl Harbor attacks which allegedly were used by the American government to bring the US into the war on the side of the communists, and the September 11 attacks, which were supposedly orchestrated by the Jews/Illuminati so as to justify an all-out war against Islam.

Appendices

The tables in this section refer to violent acts perpetrated against Jewish targets worldwide during 2001. The figures are based on the database of the Stephen Roth Institute and reports of the Coordination Forum for Countering Antisemitism.

The data in the tables are classified into two categories:

(1) Major attacks. Includes attacks and attempted attacks by violent means, such as arson, firebombs, shootings, etc.

(2) Major violent incidents. Includes harassment and vandalism of Jewish property and sites, such as damage to community buildings, desecration of synagogues and street violence not involving the use of a weapon.

It should be stressed that the numbers of incidents presented in the various tables reflect only serious acts of antisemitic violence.

VIOLENT ANTISEMITIC ACTIVITIES

Year	Major Attacks	Major Violent Incidents
1989	31	47
1990	46	132
1991	61	106
1992	48	173
1993	46	225
1994	72	232
1995	41	142
1996	32	165
1997	38	116
1998	35	121
1999	33	114
2000	66	189
2001	50	178

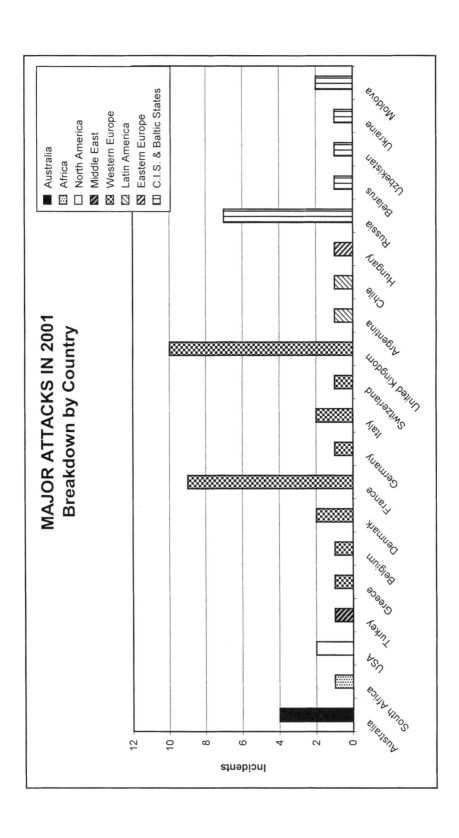

MAJOR ATTACKS IN 2001
Breakdown by Country

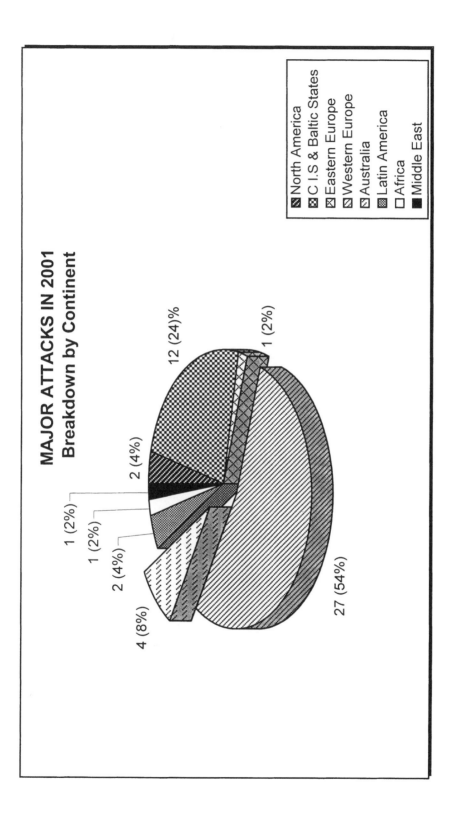

MAJOR ATTACKS IN 2001
Breakdown by Continent

12 (24)%

1 (2%)

2 (4%)

1 (2%)

1 (2%)

2 (4%)

4 (8%)

27 (54%)

North America
C.I.S & Baltic States
Eastern Europe
Western Europe
Australia
Latin America
Africa
Middle East

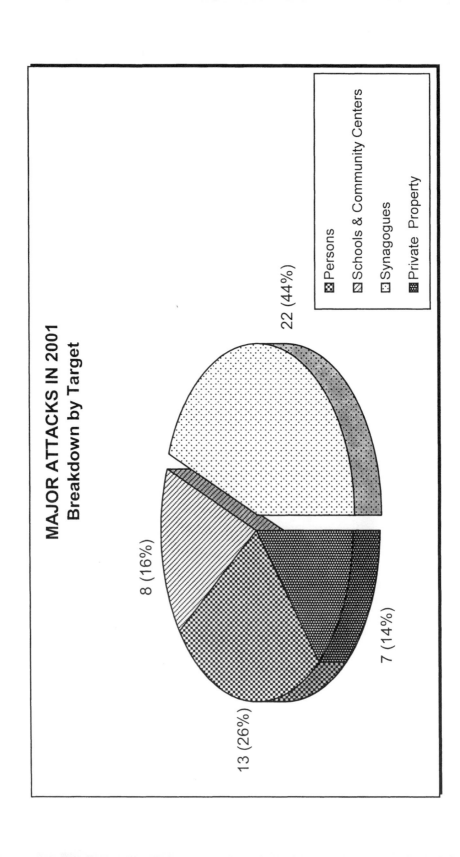

MAJOR ATTACKS IN 2001
Breakdown by Target

22 (44%)

8 (16%)

7 (14%)

13 (26%)

- Persons
- Schools & Community Centers
- Synagogues
- Private Property

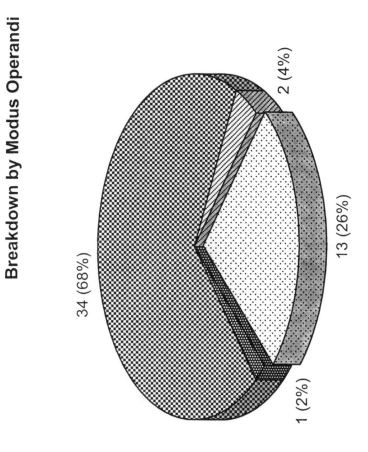

MAJOR ATTACKS IN 2001
Breakdown by Modus Operandi

34 (68%)

2 (4%)

13 (26%)

1 (2%)

- Arsons
- Explosive Devices
- Shootings / Knifings
- Deliberate Hit and Runs

MAJOR VIOLENT INCIDENTS IN 2001
Breakdown by Continent

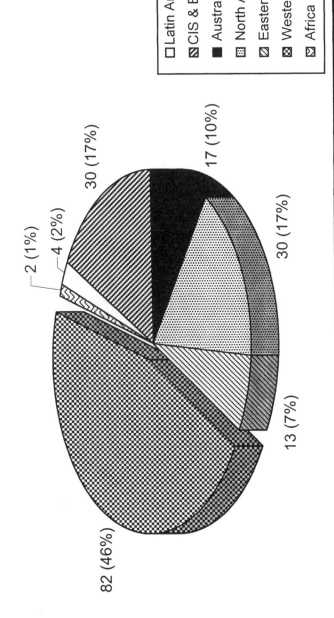

82 (46%)

2 (1%)

4 (2%)

30 (17%)

13 (7%)

17 (10%)

30 (17%)

- ☐ Latin America
- ▨ CIS & Baltic States
- ■ Australia
- ▦ North America
- ▨ Eastern Europe
- ▨ Western Europe
- ▨ Africa

MAJOR VIOLENT INCIDENTS IN 2001
Breakdown by Country

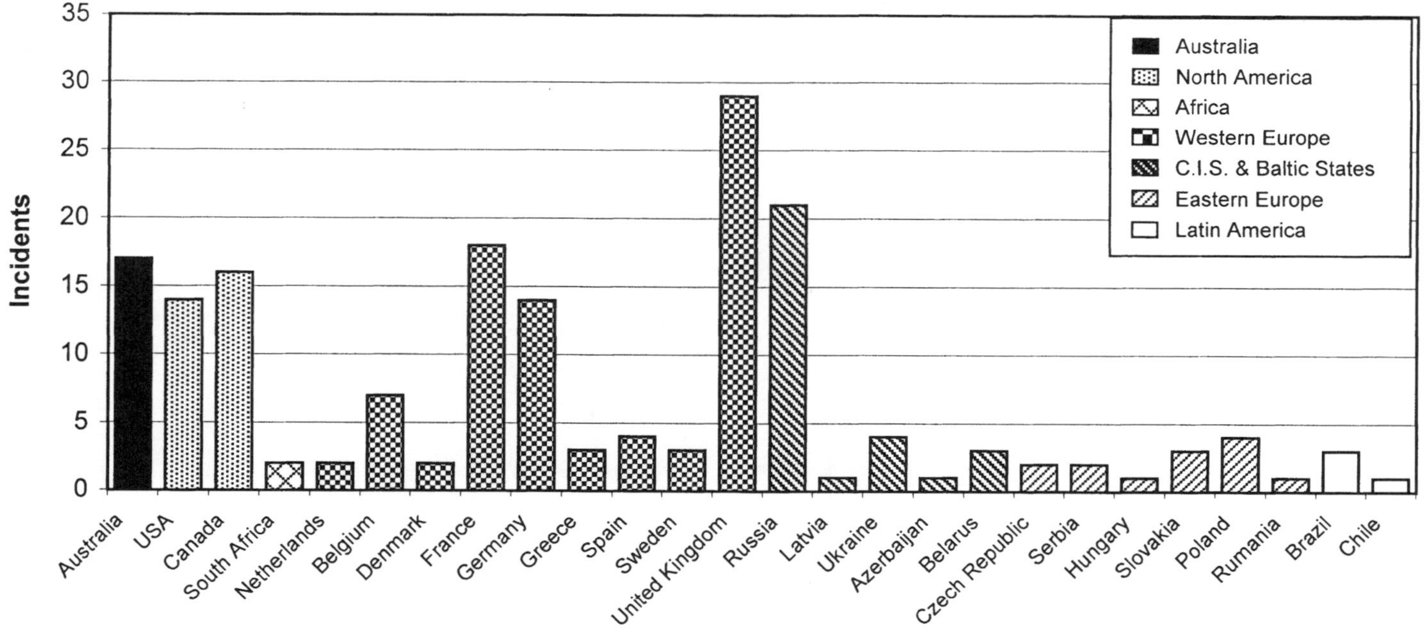

Incidents
35
30
25
20
15
10
5
0
Australia
North America
Africa
Western Europe
C.I.S. & Baltic States
Eastern Europe
Latin America
Australia
USA
Canada
South Africa
Netherlands
Belgium
Denmark
France
Germany
Greece
Spain
Sweden
United Kingdom
Russia
Latvia
Ukraine
Azerbaijan
Belarus
Czech Republic
Serbia
Hungary
Slovakia
Poland
Rumania
Brazil
Chile

MAJOR VIOLENT INCIDENTS IN 2001
Breakdown by Target

15 (8%)

44 (25%)

15 (8%)

50 (28%)

54 (31%)

Legend:
- Persons
- Schools & Community Centers
- Cemeteries & Memorials
- Synagogues
- Private Property & Businesses

- *Anti-Jewish Propaganda 1991* (1992, 305 pp., English and Hebrew; out of print).
- *Anti-Semitism in Europe in the First Quarter of 1993* (May 1993, 42 pp.; out of print).
- *Anti-Semitism in Europe in the Second Quarter of 1993* (August 1993, 91 pp.; out of print).
- *Anti-Semitism Worldwide 1993* (1994, 127 pp.).
- *Anti-Semitism Worldwide 1994* (1995, 273 pp.).
- *Anti-Semitism Worldwide 1995/6* (1996, 329 pp.).
- *Anti-Semitism Worldwide 1996/7* (1997, 372 pp.).
- *Anti-Semitism Worldwide 1997/8* (1998, 331 pp.).
- *Anti-Semitism and Extremist Movements Worldwide: Data, Characteristics and Assessments* (1998, 293 pp., Hebrew).
- *Anti-Semitism Worldwide 1998/9* (2000, 334 pp.).
- *Anti-Semitism Worldwide* 1999/2000 (2001, 286 pp.).
- *Anti-Semitism Worldwide* 2000/1 (2002, 352)

- Stephen J. Roth, The Legal Fight against Anti-Semitism. Survey of Developments in 1992 (1993, 49 pp.).
- Stephen J. Roth, *The Legal Fight against Anti-Semitism. Survey of Developments in 1993* (1995, 127 pp.).
- Raphael Vago, *Anti-Semitism in Romania*, 1989-1992 (1994, 35 pp.)
- Pierre Vidal-Naquet and Limor Yagil, *Holocaust Denial in France--Analysis of a Unique Phenomenon* (1994, 79 pp).
- Esther Webman, *Anti-Semitic Motifs in the Ideology of Hizballah and Hamas* (1994, 45 pp.).
- Robert A. Rockaway, *The Jews Cannot Defeat Me: The Anti-Jewish Campaign of Louis Farrakhan and the Nation of Islam* (November 1995, 45 pp.).
- Israel Kim, *Anti-Semitism in the United States: A National or a Locally-Based Phenomenon?* (1996, 29 pp.).
- Sarah Rembiszewski, *The Final Lie: Holocaust Denial in Germany. A Second-Generation Denier as a Test Case* (October 1996, 96 pp.).
- Jocelyn Hellig, *Anti-Semitism in South Africa* (1996, 37 pp.)
- Helene Loow, *From National Socialism to Militant Facism: The Swedish Racist Underground in the 1990s* (1996, 28 pp.).
- Mario Sznajder, Graciela Ben Dror, Esther Webman, *Extremismo y Religion su Presencia en America Latina* (1998, 80 pp.).

- Ruth Amossy, Marc Lits, *L'Image d'Israel et des Juifs durant la Guerre du Golfe--Analyse de la presse belge et francaise*. In cooperation with the University of Louvain-la-Neuve (June 1998, 89 pp.).

- Sarah Rembiszewski, *Die Leugnung des Holocaust in Deutschland: Fallstudie eines Leugners der Nachkriegsgeneration* (October 1999, 138 pp.).

- Deborah-D Emmanuel-Junod, *La Suisse et les mesures contre la discrimination raciale: l'adhesion de la Suisse a la CEDR et a la revision y relative du Code penal helvetique* (2001, 130 pp.).